*PRENTICE-HALL FOUNDATIONS OF PHILOSOPHY SERIES*

*Virgil Aldrich* — Philosophy of Art
*William Alston* — Philosophy of Language
*Stephen Barker* — Philosophy of Mathematics
*Roderick Chisholm* — Theory of Knowledge
*William Dray* — Philosophy of History
*Joel Feinberg* — Social Philosophy
*William Frankena* — Ethics
*Martin Golding* — Philosophy of Law
*Carl Hempel* — Philosophy of Natural Science
*John Hick* — Philosophy of Religion
*David Hull* — Philosophy of Biological Science
*James McClellan* — Philosophy of Education
*Willard Van Orman Quine* — Philosophy of Logic
*Richard Rudner* — Philosophy of Social Science
*Wesley Salmon* — Logic
*Jerome Shaffer* — Philosophy of Mind
*Richard Taylor* — Metaphysics

*Elizabeth and Monroe Beardsley, editors*

*second edition*

# THEORY OF KNOWLEDGE

---

Roderick M. Chisholm

BROWN UNIVERSITY

*PRENTICE-HALL, INC.*
*Englewood Cliffs, New Jersey 07632*

*Library of Congress Cataloging in Publication Data*

Chisholm, Roderick M
Theory of knowledge.

(Foundations of philosophy series)
Includes bibliographical references and index.
1. Knowledge, Theory of. I. Title.
BD161.C48 1977 121 76-43074
ISBN 0-13-914168-5
ISBN 0-13-914150-2 pbk.



10 9 8 7 6 5 4 3 2

PRENTICE-HALL INTERNATIONAL, INC., London
PRENTICE-HALL OF AUSTRALIA, PTY. LTD., Sydney
PRENTICE-HALL OF CANADA, LTD., Toronto
PRENTICE-HALL OF INDIA PRIVATE LIMITED, New Delhi
PRENTICE-HALL OF JAPAN, INC., Tokyo
PRENTICE-HALL OF SOUTHEAST ASIA PTE. LTD., Singapore
WHITEHALL BOOKS LIMITED, Wellington, New Zealand

# *FOUNDATIONS OF PHILOSOPHY*

Many of the problems of philosophy are of such broad relevance to human concerns, and so complex in their ramifications, that they are, in one form or another, perennially present. Though in the course of time they yield in part to philosophical inquiry, they may need to be rethought by each age in the light of its broader scientific knowledge and deepened ethical and religious experience. Better solutions are found by more refined and rigorous methods. Thus, one who approaches the study of philosophy in the hope of understanding the best of what it affords will look for both fundamental issues and contemporary achievements.

Written by a group of distinguished philosophers, the Foundations of Philosophy Series aims to exhibit some of the main problems in the various fields of philosophy as they stand at the present stage of philosophical history.

While certain fields are likely to be represented in most introductory courses in philosophy, college classes differ widely in emphasis, in method of instruction, and in rate of progress. Every instructor needs freedom to change his course as his own philosophical interests, the size and makeup of his classes, and the needs of his students vary from year to year. The seventeen volumes in the Foundations of Philosophy Series—each complete in itself, but complementing the others—offer a new flexibility to the instructor, who can create his own textbook by combining several volumes as he wishes, and can choose different combinations at different times. Those volumes that are not used in an introductory course will be found valuable, along with other texts or collections of readings, for the more specialized upper-level courses.

*Elizabeth Beardsley / Monroe Beardsley*

# *ACKNOWLEDGMENTS*

During the past few years I have discussed the present topics in great detail with Herbert Heidelberger and Ernest Sosa. They have contributed to this book, not only by criticizing earlier formulations, but also by making countless positive suggestions which I have followed. I regret that it is impossible to say how much of the final result is due to their help and encouragement.

I am also indebted to Alvin Plantinga for his penetrating criticisms of a preliminary version of the manuscript, and to Josiah Strandberg for his expert assistance throughout the time I have been working on the present edition of this book.

*Roderick M. Chisholm*

# CONTENTS

**INTRODUCTION**, 1

**I**

**THE TERMS OF EPISTEMIC APPRAISAL**, 5

*Epistemic Appraisal*, 5
*Some Basic Epistemic Concepts*, 7   *Certainty*, 10
*The Evident*, 11   *On Epistemic Preferability*, 12

**2**

**THE DIRECTLY EVIDENT**, 16

*Socratic Questions*, 16   *A Stopping Place?* 18
*An Improper Stopping Place*, 20
*States that Present Themselves*, 20
*The Nature of Self-presentation*, 22
*An Alternative Description*, 24
*A Skeptical Objection*, 25
*Seeming and Appearing*, 26
*Some Misconceptions*, 30

# 3

**THE TRUTHS OF REASON,** 34

*A Traditional Metaphysical View,* 34
*Not All Knowledge of Necessity Is* A Posteriori, 36
*Intuitive Induction,* 38 *Axioms,* 40
A Priori *and* A Posteriori, 46
*Skepticism with Respect to the* A Priori, 48
*"Psychologism,"* 50 *"Linguisticism,"* 53
*Analyzing the Predicate Out of the Subject,* 54
*The Synthetic* A Priori, 57
*An Untenable Dualism?* 61

# 4

**THE INDIRECTLY EVIDENT,** 62

*The Justification of the Indirectly Evident,* 62
*Beyond the Principles of Logic,* 64
*The Theory of Carneades,* 67 *Confirmation,* 71
*Perception and "Self-presentation,"* 73
*Perception and the Evident,* 77 *Memory,* 79
*Confirmation and Concurrence,* 82 *Conclusion,* 84

# 5

**TRUTH,** 87

*What Is Truth?* 87
*Assertions and Sentences as Vehicles of Truth,* 89
*The Epimenides,* 91
*Puzzles about Sentence-tokens,* 92
*Puzzles about Believing,* 95 *Pragmatism,* 97
*The True and the Evident,* 98

# 6

**KNOWLEDGE,** 102

*A Problem for the Traditional Conception of Knowledge,* 102 *A Diagnosis,* 106
*The Traditional Definition Repaired,* 109
*The Diagnosis Defended,* 111
*Knowing that One Knows,* 113
*The Right to Be Sure,* 116

7

**THE PROBLEM OF THE CRITERION,** 119

*Introduction,* 119 *Two Questions,* 120
*"Sources" of Knowledge,* 122
*"Knowledge of Right and Wrong" as One Example,* 123
*"Knowledge of External Things" as Another Example,* 126 *"Other Minds,"* 127
*A Final Example,* 132

**APPENDIX: DEFINITIONS AND PRINCIPLES,** 135

**INDEX,** 141

# Introduction

Reflection upon the nature of our knowledge gives rise to a number of perplexing philosophical problems. These constitute the subject matter of theory of knowledge, or epistemology. Most of them were discussed by the ancient Greeks and there is little agreement even now as to how they should be solved or otherwise disposed of.

The principal questions of the theory of knowledge would seem to be the following.

1. What is the distinction between knowledge and true opinion? If one man has made a lucky guess ("I would say that it is the seven of diamonds") but doesn't really know, and another man knows but isn't saying, and doesn't need to guess, what is it that the second man has (if anything) that the first man does not? One may say, of course, that the second man has *evidence* and that the first man does not, or that something is *evident* to the one that is not evident to the other. But what is it to have evidence, and how are we to decide in any particular case whether or not we do have evidence?

These questions have their analogues in both moral philosophy and logic. What is it for an act to be *right* and how are we to decide in any particular case whether or not a given act is right? What is it for an inference to be *valid* and how are we to decide in any particular case whether or not a given inference is valid?

2. Our evidence for some things, it would seem, consists of the fact that we have evidence for other things. "My evidence that he will keep his promise is the fact that he said he would keep his promise. And my evidence that he said he would keep his promise is the fact that. . . ." Must we say of everything for which we have evidence that our evidence for that thing consists in the fact that we have evidence for some other thing?

If we try Socratically to formulate our justification for any particular claim to know ("My justification for thinking that I know that *A*, is the fact that *B*"), and if we are relentless in our inquiry ("and my justification for thinking that I know that *B*, is the fact that *C*"), we will arrive, sooner or later, at a kind of stopping place ("but my justification for thinking that I know that *N*, is simply the fact that *N*"). An example of *N* might be the fact that I think that something now looks blue to me, or the fact that I seem to remember having been here before.

This type of stopping place may be described in two rather different ways. We could say, "There are some things (e.g., the fact that I seem to remember having been here before) which are evident to me and which are such that my evidence for those things does not consist in the fact that there are certain *other* things that are evident to me." Or we could say alternatively, "There are some things (e.g., the fact that I seem to remember having been here before) which cannot *themselves* be said to be evident but which resemble what can be said to be evident in that they may function as evidence *for* certain other things." These two formulations would seem to differ only verbally. If we adopt the first, we may say that some things are *directly evident*.

3. The things that we ordinarily say we *know* are not things that are thus "directly evident." But in justifying the claim to know any particular one of these things, we can be led back, in the manner described, to various things that *are* directly evident. Should we say, therefore, that the whole of what we know, at any given time, is a kind of "structure" having its "foundation" in what happens to be directly evident at that time? If we do say this, then we should be prepared to say just how it is that the foundation serves to support the rest of the structure. But this question is difficult to answer, for the support that the foundation gives would seem to be neither deductive nor inductive. That is to say, it is not the kind of support that the premises of a deductive argument give to their conclusion, nor is it the kind of support that the premises of an inductive argument give to their conclusion. For if we take as our premises the whole of what is directly evident at any time,

and if we make use of no additional premises, then we cannot formulate a good deductive argument, and we cannot formulate a good inductive argument, in which any of the things we ordinarily say we know appears as a conclusion. It may be, therefore, that in addition to the "rules of deduction" and the "rules of induction," there are also certain basic "rules of evidence." The deductive logician tries to formulate the first type of rule; the inductive logician tries to formulate the second; and the epistemologist tries to formulate the third.

4. One may ask, "*What* do we know—what is the *extent* of our knowledge?" One may also ask, "How do we decide in any particular case *whether* we know—what are the *criteria,* if any, of knowing?" The "problem of the criterion" arises out of the fact that if we do not have the answer to the second pair of questions, then, it would seem, we have no reasonable procedure for finding out the answer to the first; and if we do not have the answer to the first pair of questions, then, it would seem, we have no reasonable procedure for finding out the answer to the second. The problem may be formulated more specifically for different subject matters—for example, our knowledge (if any) of "external things," "other minds," "right and wrong," the "truths of theology." Many philosophers, apparently without sufficient reason, approach some of these more specific versions of the problem of the criterion from one point of view, and others from quite a different point of view.

5. Our knowledge (if any) of what are sometimes called the "truths of reason"—the truths of logic and mathematics and what is expressed by the statement, "A surface that is red all over is not also green"—provides us with a particularly instructive example of the problem of the criterion. Some philosophers believe that any satisfactory theory of knowledge must be adequate to the fact that some of the "truths of reason" are among the things that we know. But other philosophers formulate criteria of knowing which are such that the "truths of reason" as traditionally conceived are not among the things we know. Still others attempt to simplify the problem by saying that the so-called "truths of reason" actually pertain, somehow, only to the ways in which people think or to the ways in which they use their language. But once these suggestions are put precisely, they lose whatever plausibility they may seem at first to have.

6. The "problem of truth" may seem to be one of the simplest problems of the theory of knowledge. If we say of a man, "He believes that Socrates is mortal," and then go on to add, "And what is more, his belief is true," then what we have added, surely, is no more than that Socrates *is* mortal. And "Socrates is mortal" tells us just as much as does "It is true that Socrates is mortal." But what if we were to say of a man that some one of his beliefs is true, without specifying which

belief? What property, if any, would we be ascribing to his belief?

Suppose we say, "What he is now saying is true," when what he is now saying happens to be that what *we* are now saying is false. In this case, are we saying something that is true or are we saying something that is false?

Finally, what is the relation between conditions of truth and criteria of evidence? We have good evidence, presumably, for believing that there are nine planets. This evidence consists of various other facts that we know about astronomy, but it does not itself include the fact that there are nine planets. It would seem to be logically possible, therefore, for a man to have good evidence for a belief which is nevertheless false. Does this mean that the fact that there are nine planets, if it is a fact, is really something that cannot be evident? Should we say, therefore, that no one can really *know* that there are nine planets? Or should we say that, although it may be possible to know that there are nine planets, it is not possible to know that we know that there are nine planets? Or does the evidence that we have for believing that there are nine planets somehow guarantee that the belief is true and therefore guarantee that there are nine planets?

Such questions and problems as these constitute the subject matter of theory of knowledge. A number of them, as the reader will already feel, are simply the result of confusion; and once the confusions are exposed, the problems vanish. But others of them, as this book is intended to show, are somewhat more difficult to deal with.

This book is an attempt to present and defend one way of dealing with these questions and problems. In footnotes I have mentioned various writings representing other approaches to the subject, but for the most part I have not attempted to summarize or criticize other possible views.

CHAPTER ONE

# The Terms of Epistemic Appraisal

## 1. EPISTEMIC APPRAISAL

The theory of knowledge could be said to have as its subject matter the *justification of belief,* or, more exactly, the justification of *believing.*

The sense of "believe" that is here intended may be illustrated by contrasting a theist, an atheist, and an agnostic. The theist believes that there is a God; the atheist believes that there is no God; and the agnostic doesn't believe either of these things. We may say that what it is that the theist believes contradicts what it is that the atheist believes. And so we may also say that there is something that the theist believes and there is another thing that the atheist believes; these two things contradict each other and the agnostic doesn't believe either one of them. Using a traditional terminology, we may say that the things in question are *propositions,* one of them being the proposition that there is a God and the other being the proposition that there is no God.[1]

[1] Occasionally we will use the expression "state of affairs" in place of "proposition." The relations between propositions and states of affairs will be discussed in Chapter 5.

*What* one believes, then, is always a proposition. Hence we might characterize propositions by saying that they are the sorts of things that can be believed. They are things that *could* be objects of belief.

In what follows, it will sometimes be convenient to replace the word "believe" by the word "accept" and then to speak of the propositions that a person *accepts*. It will also be convenient to introduce the word "withhold" and say that a person *withholds* a certain proposition provided he does not accept the proposition and also does not accept the negation or contradictory of the proposition. We could then say that the agnostic withholds the proposition that there is a God, for he does not believe that there is a God and he does not believe that there is no God. And since he thus withholds the proposition that there is a God, then, *ipso facto*, he withholds the proposition that there is no God.

So far as belief is concerned, then, there are three attitudes that one may take toward a given proposition at any particular time: (1) one may believe (or accept) the proposition; (2) one may disbelieve the proposition, and this is the same thing as accepting its negation; or (3) one may withhold or suspend belief—that is to say, one may refrain from believing and from disbelieving the proposition.

Philosophical language, as well as ordinary language, frequently obscures the distinction between disbelieving and withholding. If a philosopher tells us that we should "reject" a certain proposition, he may mean that we should disbelieve it, i.e., that we should believe its negation. Or he may mean that we should withhold the proposition. And if the man in the street tells us that he "does not believe" a given proposition, he is likely to mean that he believes its negation, but he *may* mean instead that he is withholding the proposition.

What now of justification?

The term "justify," in its application to a belief, is used as a term of epistemic appraisal—a term that is used to say something about the reasonableness of belief. The term "reasonable" itself, therefore, may also be used as a term of epistemic appraisal. The same is so for such terms as "evident," "probable," "gratuitous," "certain," "unacceptable," and "indifferent." Let us begin by considering some of these terms and noting how they are related to each other.

Since they are terms of appraisal, we may best see their interrelations by introducing a comparative term—an expression that may be used to compare different beliefs with respect to reasonableness. Thus we may say that one belief is *more reasonable than* another, or, more exactly, that one belief is more reasonable for a given person at a given time than is another belief. As alternatives to "more reasonable than," we might also use "epistemically better than" or "epistemically preferable to."

Let us consider two rather clear-cut uses of "more reasonable than." The first expresses a suggestion made by St. Augustine: even though there might be ground to question the reliability of the senses, it is *more reasonable* for most of us most of the time to believe that we can safely rely upon them than to believe that we cannot.[2] The second is somewhat different: even if there is in fact life upon Venus, nevertheless, for most of us at the present time, it is more reasonable to withhold the proposition that there is life upon Venus than it is to accept it.

We may ask, then, with respect to any given proposition and any given subject at any given time, which is the most reasonable course: believing the proposition, disbelieving the proposition, or withholding the proposition? In considering such a question, we may refer to the following possibilities among others: (1) believing the proposition is more reasonable than withholding it; (2) believing it is more reasonable than disbelieving it; and (3) withholding it is more reasonable than believing it.

## 2. SOME BASIC EPISTEMIC CONCEPTS

Let us now consider what is suggested by these possibilities.

1. A proposition falling within the first category is one such that (for a given subject at a given time) believing it is more reasonable than withholding it. Any such proposition could be said to be one that is beyond reasonable doubt (for that subject at that time). Since the concept of thus being beyond reasonable doubt is one we will often use in this book, we will put our definition of it somewhat more formally as follows:

D1.1 *h* is *beyond reasonable doubt* for *S* =Df Accepting *h* is more reasonable for *S* than is withholding *h*.[3]

In this definition and others like it that will follow, we will assume that there is also a reference to some specific time. What is beyond

[2] This thesis is suggested by St. Augustine in his polemics against the skeptics. See his *Against the Academicians* (Milwaukee: Marquette University Press, 1942). The thesis is explicitly formulated by Bertrand Russell in *An Inquiry into Meaning and Truth* (New York: W. W. Norton & Company, Inc., 1940), p. 166: ". . . beliefs caused by perception are to be accepted unless there are positive grounds for rejecting them."

[3] The expression "D1.1" may be read as "the first definition in Chapter 1." For the reader's convenience, all the definitions formulated in this book are listed in the Appendix.

reasonable doubt for a given person at one time need not be beyond reasonable doubt for that person at other times.

"Beyond reasonable doubt," in the sense just defined, may be said to be a term of high epistemic praise. Of the three possibilities we have noted, this one puts the proposition in the best possible light.

The propositions that satisfy the negation of this first category—those propositions which are such that it is *not* more reasonable to believe them than it is to withhold them—may be said to be epistemically *gratuitous.* They are gratuitous for there is no need, epistemically, to accept them.

2. The second category comprises those propositions which are such that believing them is more reasonable than disbelieving them. If we say of a proposition that it falls within this category, we are expressing only faint epistemic praise. For in saying that believing is more reasonable than disbelieving we may be saying only that the former is the lesser evil, epistemically. Consider, for example, the proposition that the Pope will be in Rome on the third Tuesday in October five years from now. Believing it, given the information we now have, is more reasonable than *disbelieving* it, i.e., it is more reasonable to believe that the Pope will be in Rome at that time than it is to believe that he will *not* be there. But withholding the proposition, surely, is more reasonable still.

Let us say of any proposition thus falling within our second category that it is one having some *presumption in its favor.* Let us add this second definition:

D1.2 *h* has *some presumption in its favor* for *S* =Df Accepting *h* is more reasonable for *S* than accepting not-*h*.

The concepts defined in our first two definitions are such that the first implies the second, but not conversely. That is to say, whatever is beyond reasonable doubt is also such that it has some presumption in its favor, but some propositions having some presumption in their favor are not such that they are beyond reasonable doubt.

The negation of this second category yields a class of propositions having somewhat questionable epistemic status. The propositions belonging to this class are those which are such that believing them is *not* more reasonable than disbelieving them. These propositions, then, will be such that there is *no* presumption in their favor.

3. If we say of a proposition that it falls within our third category, we are expressing epistemic dispraise or condemnation, for we are saying of it that withholding is more reasonable than believing. We are saying "Nay"—but in the sense of "Do not believe" and not in the

sense of "Believe that not." Let us say that any proposition falling within this category is epistemically *unacceptable*.

Among the propositions that are thus unacceptable are, of course, those which are such that their negations are reasonable, in the sense of our first definition above. But the class of unacceptable propositions would seem to be considerably wider than the class of propositions that have reasonable negations. Sextus Empiricus tells us that, according to the skeptic Agrippa, "it is necessary to suspend judgment altogether with regard to *everything* that is brought before us."[4] Other, more moderate skeptics would have us suspend judgment with respect merely to those propositions that refer "beyond the appearances." But according to both types of skeptic, there are unacceptable propositions that have unacceptable negations; for example, the proposition that there are many things "beyond the appearances" is unacceptable and so is its negation. The older positivistic philosophers of the nineteenth century said of metaphysical propositions that both they and their negations are unacceptable.[5] And if what we shall say below is correct, there are still other unacceptable propositions that have unacceptable negations. Hence, although we can say that all reasonable propositions have unacceptable negations, we cannot say that all unacceptable propositions have reasonable negations.

If a proposition falls under the negation of this third category, it will be one such that withholding it is not more reasonable than believing it; hence, we may say of it that it is acceptable. We add, then, this definition:

D1.3 $h$ is *acceptable* for $S$ =Df Withholding $h$ is not more reasonable for $S$ than accepting $h$.

All propositions that are beyond reasonable doubt will, of course, be acceptable, but there are many acceptable propositions that are not beyond reasonable doubt. An adequate theory of perception, for

4 Sextus Empiricus, *Outlines of Pyrrhonism,* Book I, Chapter 15, p. 177. Epictetus, however, reminds us that believing is often more reasonable than withholding and says this of the person who accepts the skepticism of Agrippa: "He has sensation and pretends that he has not; he is worse than dead. One man does not see the battle; he is ill off. The other sees it but stirs not, nor advances; his state is still more wretched. His sense of shame and self-respect is cut out of him, and his reasoning faculty, though not cut away, is brutalized. Am I to call this 'strength'? Heaven forbid, unless I call it 'strength' in those who sin against nature, that makes them do and say in public whatever occurs to their fancy." *Discourses,* Book I, Chapter 6 ("Against Followers of the Academy"); quoted from *The Stoic and Epicurean Philosophers,* ed. Whitney J. Oates (New York: Random House, 1940), p. 233.

5 But the positivistic philosophers of the twentieth century have held that there *are* no metaphysical propositions and hence that sentences that purport to express them have no sense.

example, might require us to say this: if I have that experience which might naturally be expressed by saying that I "seem to see" a certain state of affairs (e.g., "I seem to see a man standing there"), then the state of affairs that I thus seem to perceive (the proposition that a man is standing there) is one that is, for me, *ipso facto,* acceptable. It may be, however, that although the proposition is thus acceptable, it is not beyond reasonable doubt; i.e., although withholding it is not more reasonable than believing it, believing it cannot be said to be more reasonable than withholding it. "Acceptable," then, expresses less praise than does "reasonable." But it expresses more praise than does the doubtful compliment, "Believing is more reasonable than disbelieving," which tells us merely that the proposition has *some* presumption in its favor.[6]

**3. CERTAINTY** There is epistemic praise that is even higher than "beyond reasonable doubt." For example, we may say of a proposition not only that it is beyond reasonable doubt for a man at a certain time, but also that it is *certain,* or *absolutely certain,* for that man at that time. We could say that a proposition is certain if it is beyond reasonable doubt and if it is at least as reasonable as any other proposition. Our definition, then, is this:

D1.4 *h* is *certain* for *S* =Df *h* is beyond reasonable doubt for *S,* and there is no *i* such that accepting *i* is more reasonable for *S* than accepting *h.*

The epistemic concept here defined should be distinguished from the psychological concept which might be expressed by saying, "*S* feels certain that *h* is true." The two concepts are logically independent of each other. To distinguish our epistemic sense of "certain" from the psychological concept expressed by "feels certain," we will sometimes use the expression "absolutely certain."

We have suggested that if I seem to see a man standing before me, then the proposition that there is a man standing before me is one that is for me, at that time, acceptable. But what of the proposition expressed by the words, "I *seem* to see a man standing before me"? As we

[6] Another important epistemic concept is that of a proposition being *counterbalanced.* A proposition is counterbalanced if there is as much, or as little, to be said in favor of accepting it as there is to be said in favor of accepting its negation. We may say of any such proposition that there is no presumption in its favor and also no presumption in favor of its negation. Thus we could define "*h* is counterbalanced for *S*" by saying: "Accepting *h* is not more reasonable for *S* than accepting not-*h,* and accepting not-*h* is not more reasonable for *S* than accepting *h.*" The followers of Pyrrho held that, if a proposition is counterbalanced, then it ought to be withheld. And they tried to show, as far as possible, that every proposition is counterbalanced. Compare Sextus Empiricus, *Outlines of Pyrrhonism,* Book I, Chapters 4, 6, 22, and 24.

shall see, such propositions as this, along with some of the propositions of logic and mathematics, are propositions which, at times, can be said to be absolutely certain.

## 4. THE EVIDENT

What now is the epistemic status of the ordinary things we know—the proposition, say, that the sun is now shining, or that it was shining yesterday, or that we are now in a room with other people? If we look just to the epistemic concepts that have been singled out so far, we must choose between saying either that these propositions are absolutely certain or else that they are not certain but are beyond reasonable doubt. To say that they are absolutely certain, however, would seem to be saying too much. And to say only that they are beyond reasonable doubt would seem to be saying not quite enough.

If we say that these propositions are *certain,* then we must say that no other propositions are *more* respectable epistemically than they are. For if a proposition *h* is absolutely certain for a man at a given time, then there is no proposition *i* which is such that it is more reasonable for him to believe *i* at that time than it is for him to believe *h*. But even though we *know* that the sun is now shining, that it was shining yesterday, and that we are now in a room with other people, there are propositions which are even *more* reasonable for us to believe than they are. Among these would be the elementary truths of arithmetic, or the propositions that each of us could express in English by "I exist," or indeed that it *seems* to be the case that the sun is now shining or that it shone yesterday or that there are many people in the room.

To say, then, of these ordinary things we know, that we are absolutely certain of them would seem to be saying too much. And yet it is not enough to say that these things have the status merely of being beyond reasonable doubt, i.e., of being such that it is more reasonable for us to believe them than to withhold them. There is more to be said for them than this.

Consider the building next door which is usually occupied. For most of us, the proposition that *someone or other* is now in that building is beyond reasonable doubt. But even though that proposition is now beyond reasonable doubt and even if, moreover, it is true, we don't *know* that it is true. But we *do* now know that there is someone in *this* building.

Consider another sort of example. We do now know that the man who was President of France last year was in Paris more often than not last year. And I think we can say that, for most of us, it is beyond reasonable doubt that the man who will be President of France next year will be in

Paris more often than not next year. But this latter is not a proposition that any of us now knows to be true.

When we say of a proposition that it is known to be true, then we are saying somewhat more than that it is true and beyond reasonable doubt, and we are saying somewhat less than that it is true and absolutely certain. What, then, is the epistemic status of the ordinary things we know?

One traditional term for this status is "evident," and let us use it in this connection. We will say, of the ordinary things we know, that these things are *evident*. The epistemic status of being evident is more impressive, epistemically, than that of being merely beyond reasonable doubt, and it is less impressive, epistemically, than that of being absolutely certain. What, then, do we mean by the expression "*h* is evident for *S*," and how are we to relate this concept to our other epistemic concepts?

Let us say that an evident proposition is a proposition which is beyond reasonable doubt and which is such that any proposition that is more reasonable than it is one that is certain. In other words:

D1.5 *h* is evident for *S* =Df (i) *h* is beyond reasonable doubt for *S* and (ii) for every *i*, if accepting *i* is more reasonable for *S* than accepting *h*, then *i* is certain for *S*.

This definition presupposes that being evident, like being certain, is not capable of degrees.

Although, as we have said, a proposition may be evident and yet not absolutely certain, we may assume that every proposition that is absolutely certain is also one that is evident.

## 5. ON EPISTEMIC PREFERABILITY

We have been trying to explicate some of the basic concepts of the theory of knowledge. It is obvious that, if we are able to explicate any given concept, we can do so only by making use of certain other concepts. Or, to put the matter in a somewhat different way, if we are able to define any given expression, we can do so only by making use of other expressions that we do not define. We have been using the undefined technical expression, "*p* is more reasonable than *q* for *S* at *t*" (or, alternatively put, "*p* is epistemically preferable to *q* for *S* at *t*"). Can we throw any light upon this undefined expression?

There are two ways of throwing light upon what is intended by an undefined expression. One is to make explicit the basic principles it is used to formulate. The other is to try to paraphrase the undefined expression into a different terminology. Let us consider each of these two procedures.

What basic principles may be formulated as axioms of the concept expressed by "more reasonable than"? Another way of putting the question is to ask: What are the basic principles of epistemic logic, or the logic of epistemic appraisal? Among these principles, I suggest, are the following four:

1. *More reasonable than* is an intentional concept: If believing one proposition is more reasonable than believing another for any given subject *S*, then *S* is at least able to *understand* or *grasp* the first proposition. It follows from this that only rational beings—things that are capable of understanding—are such that, for them, some propositions are more reasonable than others. It also follows that, if a proposition has positive epistemic status for a given subject *S*, that is to say, if it is such that for *S* it has some presumption in its favor, or is acceptable, or is beyond reasonable doubt, or is evident, or is certain, then it is a proposition that *S* understands.

2. *More reasonable than* is a transitive relation: If one thing is more reasonable than another and the other more reasonable than a third, then the first thing is more reasonable than the third. Thus if for a given subject believing a certain proposition *h* is more reasonable than disbelieving a certain other proposition *i*, and if disbelieving *i* is more reasonable than withholding still another proposition *j*, then believing *h* is more reasonable than withholding *j*.

3. *More reasonable than* is also asymmetrical: If one thing is more reasonable for one subject than another, then the other is not more reasonable for him than the one. Thus if withholding a proposition is more reasonable than believing it, then believing it is not more reasonable than withholding it.

4. And, finally, if withholding is not more reasonable than believing, then believing is more reasonable than disbelieving. Or, more exactly, for any proposition *h* and any subject *S*, if it is not more reasonable for *S* to withhold *h* than it is for him to believe *h*, then it is more reasonable for *S* to believe *h* than it is for him to disbelieve *h*. An instance of this principle would be: if agnosticism is not more reasonable than theism, then theism is more reasonable than atheism.[7]

[7] For a formal epistemic system in which the last three of these principles appear, see Roderick M. Chisholm and Robert Keim, "A System of Epistemic Logic," *Ratio*, XV (1973), 99–115. The third and fourth principles above are there taken as axioms; the second is replaced by the stronger principle according to which the relation expressed by "not epistemically preferable" (or "not more reasonable than") is transitive. There are four other axioms in that system which may be suggested by the following informal statements: "Believing *h* is preferable to believing *i*, if and only if, believing

We have said that there is a second way of making clear what is intended by an undefined expression. This way is to try to paraphrase that expression into a different terminology.

Let us consider the concept of what might be called an "intellectual requirement." We may assume that every person is subject to a purely intellectual requirement—that of trying his best to bring it about that, for every proposition *h* that he considers, he accepts *h* if and only if *h* is true.[8] One might say that this is the person's responsibility or duty *qua* intellectual being. (But as a requirement it is only a *prima facie* duty; it may be, and usually is, overridden by others, nonintellectual requirements, and it may be fulfilled more or less adequately.[9]) One way, then, of re-expressing the locution "*p* is more reasonable than *q* for *S* at *t*" is to say this: "*S* is so situated at *t* that his intellectual requirement, his responsibility as an intellectual being, is better fulfilled by *p* than by *q*."

One might ask: "So far as our purely intellectual requirements are concerned, isn't the proper thing always to play it safe and restrict our beliefs to those propositions that are absolutely certain?" The following observation by William James reminds us that, even if one is subject only to purely intellectual requirements, one should not be motivated *merely* by the desire to play it safe: "There are two ways of looking at our duty in the matter of opinion—ways entirely different, and yet ways about whose difference the theory of knowledge seems hitherto to have shown very little concern. We *must know the truth:* and we *must avoid error*—these are our first and great commandments as would-be knowers; but they are not two ways of stating an identical commandment, they are two separable laws."[10]

---

not-*i* is preferable to believing not-*h*"; "Withholding *h* is the same in epistemic value as withholding *i,* if and only if, either believing *h* is the same in epistemic value as believing *i* or believing not-*h* is the same in epistemic value as believing *i*" (two propositions are the same in epistemic value if neither one is epistemically preferable to the other); "If believing *i* is preferable to believing *h* and also preferable to believing not-*h,* then withholding *h* is preferable to withholding *i*"; and "Withholding *h* is the same as withholding not-*h.*" Compare also Philip L. Quinn, "Some Epistemic Implications of 'Crucial Experiments,'" *Studies in the History and Philosophy of Science,* V (1975), 59–72; and Robert Keim, "Epistemic Values and Epistemic Viewpoints," in *Analysis and Metaphysics,* ed., Keith Lehrer (Dordrecht: D. Reidel, 1975), pp. 75–92.

[8] See J. T. Stevenson, "On Doxastic Responsibility," in *Analysis and Metaphysics,* ed. Lehrer, pp. 229–253.

[9] I have discussed the concept of requirement in detail in "Practical Reason and the Logic of Requirement," in *Practical Reason,* ed. Stephen Körner (Oxford: Basil Blackwell, 1974), pp. 40–53. The concepts of *overriding,* of *prima facie duty,* and of *absolute duty* are there defined in terms of requirement.

[10] William James, *The Will to Believe and Other Essays in Popular Philosophy* (New York: David McKay Co., Inc., 1911), p. 17.

Each person, then, is subject to two quite different requirements in connection with any proposition he considers: (1) he should try his best to bring it about that if that proposition is true then he believe it; and (2) he should try his best to bring it about that if that proposition is false then he not believe it. Each requirement by itself would be quite simple: to fulfill the first, our purely intellectual being could simply believe *every* proposition that comes along; to fulfill the second, he could *refrain* from believing *any* proposition that comes along. To fulfill both is more difficult. If he had only the second requirement—that of trying his best to bring it about that if a proposition is false then he not believe that proposition—then he could always play it safe and never act at all, doxastically. But sometimes more than just playing it safe is necessary if he is also to fulfill the first requirement: that of trying his best, with respect to the propositions he considers, to believe the ones that are true.

Obviously there are some *true* propositions which are such that it is more reasonable, for us now, to withhold those propositions than it is for us to believe them.

And are there some *false* propositions which are such that it is more reasonable, for us now, to believe those propositions than it is for us to withhold them? We will find that this may well be true. Or, more exactly, we will find that, if the skeptics are mistaken and if, as a matter of fact, we know pretty much the things about the world that we now think we know, then it is quite possible that some false propositions are such that it is more reasonable for us to believe those propositions than it is for us to withhold them.

Indeed, we will find this: it is possible that there are some propositions which are both *evident* and false.[11] This fact makes the theory of knowledge more difficult than it otherwise would be and it has led some philosophers to wonder whether, after all, the things we know might not be restricted to those things that are absolutely certain. (For we will not find it possible that what is absolutely certain might be false.) But if we do in fact know most of those ordinary things that we think we know (that there are such and such pieces of furniture in the room, that the sun was shining yesterday, that the earth, as G. E. Moore put it, has existed for many years past), then we must reconcile ourselves to the possibility that on occasion some of those things that are evident to us are also false.

This possibility will be clear when we consider the indirectly evident. But first we will consider the directly evident.

[11] It may be that Pierre Bayle was the first to call attention to this fact. See his *Historical and Critical Dictionary: Selections,* ed. Richard H. Popkin (Indianapolis: Bobbs-Merrill Company, Inc., 1965), pp. 199–201.

## CHAPTER TWO

# The Directly Evident

One says "I know" when one is ready to give compelling grounds. "I know" relates to a possibility of demonstrating the truth. Whether someone knows something can come to light, assuming that he is convinced of it. But if what he believes is of such a kind that the grounds that he can give are no surer than his assertion, then he cannot say that he knows what he believes.

LUDWIG WITTGENSTEIN[1]

The nature of the good can be learned from experience only if the content of experience be first classified into good and bad, or grades of better and worse. Such classification or grading already involves the legislative application of the same principle which is sought. In logic, principles can be elicited by generalization from examples only if cases of valid reasoning have first been segregated by some criterion. It is this criterion which the generalization is required to disclose. In esthetics, the laws of the beautiful may be derived from experience only if the criteria of beauty have first been correctly applied.

C. I. LEWIS[2]

### 1. SOCRATIC QUESTIONS

In investigating the theory of evidence from a philosophical—or Socratic—point of view, we make three general presuppositions.

We presuppose, first, that there *is* something that we know and we adopt the working hypothesis that *what* we know is pretty much that which, on reflection, we think we know. This may seem the wrong place to start. But where else *could* we start? (We will consider some alternatives in the final chapter.)

[1] *On Certainty* (Oxford: Basil Blackwell, 1969), p. 32e.

[2] *Mind and the World-Order* (New York: Charles Scribner's Sons, 1929), p. 29; cf. his discussion of the "critique of cogency," in *The Ground and Nature of the Right* (New York: Columbia University Press, 1955), pp. 20–38.

We presuppose, second, that the things we know are justified for us in the following sense: *we* can know what it is, on any occasion, that constitutes our grounds, or reason, or evidence for thinking that we know. If I think that I know that there is now snow on the top of the mountain, then, as the quotation from Wittgenstein suggests, I am in a position to say what ground or reason I have for thinking that there is now snow on the top of the mountain. (Of course, from the fact that there *is* ground for thinking that there is now snow there, from the fact, say, that you have been there and seen it, it doesn't follow that *I* now have any ground or reason for the belief.)

And we presuppose, third, that if we do thus have grounds or reasons for the things we think we know, then there are valid general principles of evidence—principles stating the general conditions under which we may be said to have grounds or reasons for what we believe. And, as the quotation from Lewis above suggests, our concern, in investigating the theory of evidence, is to find out what these general principles are.

In order to formulate, or make explicit, our rules of evidence, we will do well to proceed as we do in logic, when formulating the rules of inference, or in moral philosophy, when formulating rules of action. We suppose that we have at our disposal certain instances which the rules should countenance or permit and other instances which the rules should reject or forbid; and we suppose that by investigating these instances we can formulate criteria which any instance must satisfy if it is to be accepted or permitted, as well as criteria which any instance must satisfy if it is to be rejected or forbidden. To obtain the instances we need if we are to formulate rules of evidence, we may proceed in the following way.

We consider certain things that we know to be true, or think we know to be true, or certain things which, upon reflection, we would be willing to call *evident*. With respect to each of these, we then try to formulate a reasonable answer to the question, "What justification do you have for thinking you know this thing to be true?" or "What justification do you have for counting this thing as something that is evident?" In beginning with what we think we know to be true, or with what, after reflection, we would be willing to count as being evident, we are assuming that the truth we are seeking is "already implicit in the mind which seeks it, and needs only to be elicited and brought to clear reflection."[3]

There are philosophers who point out, with respect to some things that are quite obviously known to be true, that questions concerning their justification "do not arise," for (they say) to express a doubt concerning such things is to "violate the rules of our language." But their

[3] Lewis, *Mind and the World-Order*, p. 19.

objections do not apply to the type of question that we are discussing here; for these questions need not be taken to express any doubts or to indicate any attitude of skepticism. Designed only to elicit information, the questions are not challenges and they do not imply or presuppose that there is any ground for doubting, or for suspecting, that to which they pertain.[4] When Aristotle considered an invalid mood and asked himself "What is wrong with this?" he was trying to learn; he need not have been suggesting to himself that perhaps nothing was wrong with the mood.

It should be also noted that when we ask ourselves, concerning what we may think we know to be true, "What *justification* do I have for believing this?" or "What justification do I have for thinking I know that this is something that is true?" we are not asking any of the following questions: "What *further evidence* can I find in support of this?" "How did I *come to believe* this or find out that it is true?" "How would I go about *persuading* some other reasonable person that it is true?" We must not expect, therefore, that answers to these latter questions will be, *ipso facto,* answers to the questions that we are asking. Our questions are Socratic and therefore not at all of the type that one ordinarily asks.[5]

## 2. A STOPPING PLACE?

In many instances the answers to our questions will take the following form: "What justifies me in thinking that I know that *a* is *F* is the fact that it is evident to me that *b* is *G*." For example: "What justifies me in thinking I know that he has that disorder is the fact that it is evident to me that he has those symptoms." Such an answer, therefore, presup-

[4] These remarks also apply to Leonard Nelson's statement, "If one asks whether one possesses objectively valid cognitions at all, one thereby presupposes that the objectivity of cognition is questionable at first . . ."; *Socratic Method and Critical Philosophy* (New Haven: Yale University Press, 1949), p. 190. One of the unfortunate consequences of the work of Descartes and, in the present century, the work of Bertrand Russell and Edmund Husserl, is the widely accepted supposition that questions about the justification for counting evident statements *as* evident must be *challenges* or expressions of *doubts.* See Bertrand Russell's *Problems of Philosophy* (New York: Holt Rinehart & Winston, Inc., 1912) and his many other writings on the theory of knowledge, and E. Husserl's *Meditations Cartesiennes* (Paris: J. Vrin, 1931), also published as *Cartesianische Meditationen und Pariser Vorträge* (The Hague: Martinus Nijhoff, 1950). The objections to this approach to the concept of the evident were clearly put forth by A. Meinong; see his *Gesammelte Abhandlungen,* II (Leipzig: Johann Ambrosius Barth, 1913), p. 191. The papers by Nelson and Meinong that are here referred to are reprinted in *Empirical Knowledge: Readings from Contemporary Sources,* Roderick M. Chisholm and Robert J. Swartz, eds. (Englewood Cliffs, N.J.: Prentice-Hall, Inc., 1973).

[5] According to Xenophon, Charicles said to Socrates: "You generally ask questions when you know quite well how the matter stands; these are the questions you are not to ask." [*Memorabilia,* I, 2, 36]

poses an epistemic principle, what we might call a "rule of evidence." The rule would have the form:

If it is evident to me that *b* is *G*, then it is evident to me that *a* is *F*.

"If it *is* evident that he has those symptoms, then it is also evident that he has that disorder." And so we should distinguish the answer to our Socratic question from its epistemic presupposition. The answer to our Socratic question is a proposition to the effect that our justification for counting one thing as evident is the fact that something else is evident. And the epistemic presupposition of our answer is a rule of evidence: It is a proposition to the effect that if certain conditions obtain, then something may be said to be evident. One could say of such a rule that it tells us that one thing *serves to make another thing evident.*

This type of answer to our Socratic questions shifts the burden of justification from one claim to another. For we may now ask, "What justifies me in counting it as evident that *b* is *G*?" or "What justifies me in thinking I know that *b* is *G*?" And possibly we will formulate, once again, an answer of the first sort: "What justifies me in counting it as evident that *b* is *G* is the fact that it is evident that *c* is *H*." ("What justifies me in counting it as evident that he has those symptoms is the fact that it is evident that his temperature is recorded as being high. . . .") And this answer will presuppose still another rule of evidence: "If it is evident that *c* is *H*, then it is evident that *b* is *G*." How long can we continue in this way?

We might try to continue *ad indefinitum*, justifying each new claim that we elicit by still another claim. Or we might be tempted to complete a vicious circle: in such a case, having justified "*a* is *F*" by appeal to "*b* is *G*," and "*b* is *G*" by reference to "*c* is *H*," we would then justify "*c* is *H*" by reference to "*a* is *F*." But if we are rational beings, we will do neither of these things. For we will find that our Socratic questions lead us to a proper stopping place.

How are we to recognize such a stopping place?

Sextus Empiricus remarked that every object of apprehension seems to be apprehended either through itself or through another object.[6] Those things, if there are any, that are "apprehended through themselves" might provide us with a stopping place. But what could they be? The form of our Socratic questions suggests a way of finding an answer. Let us say provisionally that we have found a proper stopping place when the answer to our question may take the following form:

What justifies me in thinking I know that *a* is *F* is simply the fact that *a* is *F*.

[6] Sextus Empiricus, *Outlines of Pyrrhonism,* Book I, Chapter 6, in *Sextus Empiricus,* Vol. I, The Loeb Classical Library (Cambridge: Harvard University Press, 1933).

Whenever this type of answer is appropriate, we have encountered what is *directly evident.*

### 3. AN IMPROPER STOPPING PLACE

At first consideration, one might suppose that those statements that correctly describe our "experience," or formulate our "perceptions" or "observations," are statements expressing what is directly evident in the sense described. But what is expressed by such statements does not satisfy the criteria we have just set forth.

In answer to the question, "What is my justification for thinking I know that Mr. Smith is here?" one may say, "I see that he is here." But "I see that he is here" does not pick out the kind of stopping place we have just described in reply to the question, "What is my justification for counting it as evident that it is Mr. *Smith* that I see?" A reasonable man will *not* say, "What justifies me in counting it as evident that I see Mr. Smith is simply the fact that I do see Mr. Smith." If he understands the Socratic question, he will say instead something like: "I know that Mr. Smith is a tall man with red hair; I see a tall man with red hair; I know that no one else satisfying that description would be in this room now. . . ." Each of these propositions in turn, including "I see a tall man with red hair," would be justified by reference to still other propositions. And this is true of any other perceptual proposition. Hence, we cannot say that what we know by means of perception or observation is itself something that is directly evident.

There are those who will say, "What justifies me in counting it as evident that Mr. Smith is here (or that I see Mr. Smith) is simply my present *experience;* but the experience itself cannot be said to be evident, much less to have evidence conferred upon it." But this reply seems clearly to make room for further Socratic questioning. For we may ask, "What justifies me in counting it as evident that my experience is of such a sort that experiences of that sort make it evident to me that Mr. Smith is here, or that I see that Mr. Smith is here?" And to this question one could reasonably reply in the way described above.

### 4. STATES THAT PRESENT THEMSELVES

The following quotation from Leibniz points to what is directly evident: "Our direct awareness of our own existence and of our own thoughts provides us with the primary truths *a posteriori,* the primary truths of fact, or, in other words, our primary experiences; just as identical propositions constitute the primary truths *a priori,* the primary truths of reason, or, in other words, our primary insights. Neither the one nor the other is capable of being demonstrated and both can be called *immediate*—the former, because there is no mediation between the understanding and its objects, and the latter because there is no mediation between the subject and the predicate."[7] We are here concerned with Leibniz's "primary truths of fact." The "primary truths of reason" will be discussed in the next chapter.

Thinking and believing provide us with paradigm cases of the directly evident. Consider a reasonable man who is thinking about a city he takes to be Albuquerque, or who believes that Albuquerque is in New Mexico, and suppose him to reflect on the philosophical question, "What is my justification for thinking that I know that I am thinking about a city I take to be Albuquerque, or that I believe that Albuquerque is in New Mexico?" (This strange question would hardly arise, of course, on any practical occasion, for the man is not asking, "What is my justification for thinking that Albuquerque is in New Mexico?" The question is a Socratic question and therefore a philosophical one.) The man could reply in this way: "My justification for thinking I know that I am thinking about a city I take to be Albuquerque, or that I believe that Albuquerque is in New Mexico, is simply the fact that I *am* thinking about a city I take to be Albuquerque, or that I *do* believe that it is in New Mexico." And this reply fits our formula for the directly evident:

What justifies me in thinking I know that *a* is *F* is simply the fact that *a* is *F*.

Our man has stated his justification for a proposition merely by reiterating that proposition. This type of justification is *not* appropriate to the questions that were previously discussed. Thus, in answer to "What justification do you have for counting it as evident that there can be no life on the moon?" it would be inappropriate—and presumptuous—simply to reiterate, "There can be no life on the moon." But we can state our justification for certain propositions about our *beliefs*, and certain propositions about our thoughts, merely by reiterating those propositions. They may be said, therefore, to pertain to what is directly evident.

Borrowing a technical term from Meinong, let us say that if there is something that is directly evident to a man, then there is some state of affairs that "presents itself to him." Thus, my believing that Socrates is mortal is a state of affairs that is "self-presenting" to me. If I do be-

[7] G. W. Leibniz, *New Essays Concerning Human Understanding* (La Salle, Ill.: Open Court Publishing Company, 1916), Book IV, Chapter 9.

lieve that Socrates is mortal, then, *ipso facto,* it is evident to me that I believe that Socrates is mortal; the state of affairs is "apprehended through itself."[8]

Other states that may be similarly self-presenting are those described by "thinking that one remembers that . . ." or "seeming to remember that . . ." (as distinguished from "remembering that . . ."), and "taking" or "thinking that one perceives" (as distinguished from "perceiving"). Desiring, hoping, wondering, wishing, loving, hating may also be self-presenting. These states are what Leibniz intended by the term "thoughts" in the passage quoted above.

## 5. THE NATURE OF SELF-PRESENTATION

Let us now try to characterize self-presentation more exactly. If seeming to have a headache is a state of affairs that is self-presenting for *S* at the present moment, then *S* does now seem to have a headache and, moreover, it is evident to him that he seems to have a headache.[9] And so we may formulate the definition this way:

D2.1 *h* is *self-presenting* for *S* at *t* =Df *h* occurs at *t;* and necessarily, if *h* occurs at *t,* then *h* is evident for *S* at *t.*

An alternative formulation would be this:

> *h* is self-presenting for *S* at *t* =Df *h* is true at *t;* and necessarily, if *h* is true at *t,* then *h* is evident for *S* at *t.*

The difference between the two types of formulation will be discussed in Chapter 5. For the moment, we will assume that they are interchangeable, sometimes saying that *states of affairs* are what is self-presenting and at other times saying that *propositions* are what is self-presenting.

We should note that what follows logically from what is self-present-

[8] See A. Meinong, *On Emotional Presentation,* ed. and trans. M. S. Kalsi (Evanston: Northwestern University Press, 1972), sec. 1. Cf. Franz Brentano, *Psychology from an Empirical Standpoint* (London: Routledge & Kegan Paul, 1972), Chapter 2, sec. 2; C. J. Ducasse, "Propositions, Truth, and the Ultimate Criterion of Truth," *Philosophy and Phenomenological Research,* IV (1944), 317–340; William J. Alston, "Varieties of Privileged Access," in *Empirical Knowledge,* Chisholm and Swartz, eds., pp. 376–410; and Thomas J. Steel, "Knowledge and the Self-Presenting," in *Analysis and Metaphysics,* ed. Keith Lehrer (Dordrecht: D. Reidel, 1975), pp. 145–150.

[9] For other approaches to the concept of self-presentation, compare: Roderick Firth, "The Anatomy of Certainty," in *Empirical Knowledge,* Chisholm and Swartz, eds., pp. 203–223; Wilfrid Sellars, "Givenness and Explanatory Coherence," *Journal of Philosophy,* LXX (1973), 612–624; and Alston, "Varieties of Privileged Access," referred to above.

ing need not itself be self-presenting. It will be instructive to consider three different examples of this fact.

1. The proposition expressed by "I seem to have a headache" logically implies that expressed by "2 and 2 are 4." But even if the former is self-presenting, the latter is not. For the latter is not necessarily such that if it is true then it is evident for me; it could be true even if I didn't exist.

2. The proposition expressed by "I seem to have a headache" logically implies that expressed by "Either I seem to have a headache or all crows are black." But the latter proposition is not necessarily such that if it is true then it is evident to me; it could be true even if I didn't exist.

3. The proposition expressed by "I seem to have a headache" logically implies that expressed by "I exist." But the latter proposition is not necessarily such that if it is true then it is evident for me; it could be true if I were asleep and such that nothing is evident to me.

The negations of self-presenting propositions will not be self-presenting, for they may all be true when no one exists and hence when nothing is evident. What of the proposition expressed by "I am thinking but I do not seem to see a dog." Is this necessarily such that, if it is true, then it is evident? No. For it could be true, even though I didn't have the concept of a dog and therefore didn't understand the proposition "I am thinking but I do not seem to see a dog." But if the proposition is one that could be true when I didn't understand it, then it is one that could be true without being evident to me. For, according to what we said in the previous chapter, a proposition cannot be evident to a person unless it is one that he is able to grasp or to understand. (More exactly, we said that, if believing one proposition is more reasonable than believing another for any given person *S*, then *S* is able to grasp or understand the first proposition.)

One may object: "But isn't it directly evident to me now both that I am thinking and that I do not see a dog?" The answer is yes. But the concept of the directly evident is not the same as that of the self-presenting.

## 6. A DEFINITION OF THE DIRECTLY EVIDENT

The concept of the directly evident is considerably broader than that of the self-presenting. A self-presenting state of affairs for *S* is one which is necessarily such that, if it occurs, then it is evident to *S*. Hence we could say that the Cartesian statement "I am thinking" expresses what is self-presenting for *S*—provided he *is* thinking. For it would be impossible for *S* to be thinking unless it were evident to him that he was thinking. But what of the statement "There is someone who is thinking"? If we adhere to the tradition of Descartes and Leibniz, we will want to say that, if "I am thinking" expresses what is directly evident for *S*, then so, too, does "There is someone who is thinking." But the latter is not self-presenting by our definition above. For it is not *necessary* that, if there is someone who is thinking, then that fact is then evident to S. (If someone is thinking while *S* is asleep, the fact that someone is thinking need not be evident to *S*.) But, we may assume, it is not possible for anyone to accept the proposition he would express by "I am thinking" unless he also accepts the proposition that someone is thinking. And so let us say:

D2.2 *h* is *directly evident* for *S* =Df *h* is logically contingent; and there is an *e* such that (i) *e* is self-presenting for *S* and (ii) necessarily, whoever accepts *e* accepts *h*.

Those propositions which are themselves self-presenting, of course, will also be directly evident by this definition.

What of *negative* propositions? Isn't it directly evident to me that I do not now seem to see a dog? If such propositions were never directly evident, it would be difficult to see what would ever justify any contingent judgments of nonexistence. Yet we noted above that "I do not now seem to see a dog" cannot be said to be self-presenting—for it may be true without being evident. From what self-presenting proposition, then, may one deduce the proposition expressed by "I do not now seem to see a dog?" The answer would seem to be this: "I am considering the proposition that I seem to see a dog, and I do not seem to see a dog." (This example illustrates the fact that negative apprehension is more complex than positive apprehension.)

## 7. AN ALTERNATIVE DESCRIPTION

"Surely," one may object, "it makes no sense to speak of evidence in the kind of cases you describe. What sense does it make to ask whether or not it is *evident* to me that I believe that Socrates is mortal?"[10]

To one who feels that such questions "make no sense," we need not reply by trying to show him that they do. It is enough to make two points: (1) If he is right, then such propositions as "I believe that Socrates is mortal" and "I am thinking about the moon" differ in one very important respect from such propositions as "Socrates is mortal" and "There can be no life on the moon." The former propositions, if

[10] Compare John V. Canfield, "'I Know that I Am in Pain' Is Senseless," in *Analysis and Metaphysics,* ed. Keith Lehrer, pp. 129–144.

our critic is right, are such that it "makes no sense" to ask, with respect to them, "What is my justification for thinking I know that they are true?" (2) Yet they resemble propositions which *are* known to be true in that they may function as *evidence*. My evidence that you and I think alike with respect to the mortality of Socrates cannot consist solely of the evidence I have concerning *your* beliefs about Socrates. It must also consist of the fact that *I* believe that Socrates is mortal. And these two points provide us with an alternative way of characterizing the directly evident.

We could say paradoxically that a proposition is *directly evident* to a man, provided (1) that it makes no sense to say of him that he knows the proposition to be true, and (2) that the proposition is evidence for him of something else.

If we use our original characterization of the directly evident, we might think of the directly evident as that which "constitutes its own evidence," for we have characterized it in terms of what is self-presenting—in terms of that which is "apprehended through itself." But if we use the alternative characterization, we may think paradoxically of the directly evident as being that which is "evidence but not evident."[11] In the one case, we are reminded of the prime mover that moves itself, and in the other, of the prime mover unmoved.[12]

It will be convenient to continue with the terms of our original characterization, but what we shall say can readily be translated into those of the second.

## 8. A SKEPTICAL OBJECTION

Before listing still other types of self-presenting states, we should consider an objection that might be made to *any* item on our list.

We have said, for example, that seeming to have a headache is self-presenting. Suppose now the skeptic asks: "But how do you *know* that seeming to have a headache is self-presenting? How do you *know* that seeming to have a headache is necessarily such that, if you do seem to have a headache, then it is evident to you that you do?"

One possible move—and one that would please the skeptic—would

11 The second method of characterization is in the spirit of the following observations by Ludwig Wittgenstein: (1) "It can't be said of me at all (except perhaps as a joke) that I *know* I'm in pain" and (2) "Justification by experience comes to an end. If it did not it would not be justification." *Philosophical Investigations* (Oxford: Basil Blackwell, 1953), pp. 89e, 136e. From the fact that it can't be said of me that I know that I'm in pain, it will not follow, of course, that it *can* be said of me that I do *not* know—i.e., that I am ignorant of the fact—that I am in pain.

12 Compare Rudolf Haller, "Concerning the So-called 'Munchhausen Trilemma,'" *Ratio,* XVI (1974), 119–140.

be this. We would try to think of some *additional* feature of self-presenting states, some feature the presence of which would guarantee us that a given state *is* a self-presenting state. And then we would go on to note that this feature is shared by such self-presenting states as seeming to have a headache and believing that all men are mortal.

But whatever features we might thus find—let us call it "*F*"—the skeptic will be ready with his answer: "But how do you know that only self-presenting states have *F*? And how do you know that seeming to have a headache and believing that all men are mortal have *F*?"

And if we were foolish enough to take on these additional questions, then the skeptic would be ready for us once again: "Yes, but how do you know . . . ?

To the questions "How do you know that you seem to have a headache?" and "How do you know that you believe that all men are mortal?" the only possible answers are, "I do seem to have a headache" and "I do believe that all men are mortal." And to the philosophical questions "How do you know that seeming to have a headache is self-presenting?" and "How do you know that believing that all men are mortal is self-presenting?" the only possible answers are, "I know that seeming to have a headache is self-presenting" and "I know that believing that all men are mortal is self-presenting."[13]

One would like to think that there is a better way of dealing with the skeptic's objection. But what could it possibly be? We will return to this general problem in the final chapter.

**9. SEEMING AND APPEARING**

We have yet to consider the most interesting—and controversial—examples of the directly evident.

In the second of his *Meditations,* Descartes offers what he takes to be good reasons for doubting whether, on any occasion, he sees light, hears noise, or feels heat, and he then observes: "Let it be so, still it is at least quite *certain that it seems to me that* I see light, that I hear noise, and that I feel heat."[14] This observation about seeming should

[13] See Franz Brentano, *Psychology from an Empirical Standpoint,* pp. 139–140. Compare Leonard Nelson's *Uber das sogenannte Erkenntnisproblem* (Göttingen: Verlag "Offentliches Leben," 1930), reprinted from *Abhandlungen der Fries'schen Schule, II* (Göttingen: Verlag "Offentliches Leben," 1908), especially pp. 479–485, 502–503, 521–524, 528. Compare "The Impossibility of the 'Theory of Knowledge,'" in his *Socratic Method and Critical Philosophy,* and reprinted in *Empirical Knowledge,* Chisholm and Swartz, eds.

[14] E. S. Haldane and G. R. T. Ross, eds., *The Philosophical Works of Descartes,* I (London: Cambridge University Press, 1934), p. 153 [my italics]. The French reads: ". . . il est certain qu'il me semble que je vois de la lumière, que j'entend du bruit et que je sens de la chaleur."

be contrasted with what St. Augustine says, in his *Contra Academicos,* about appearing.

> I do not see how the Academician can refute him who says: "I know that this appears white to me, I know that my hearing is delighted with this, I know that this has an agreeable odor, I know that this tastes sweet to me, I know that this feels cold to me." . . . I say this that, when a person tastes something, he can honestly swear that he knows it is sweet to his palate or the contrary, and that no trickery of the Greeks can dispossess him of that knowledge.[15]

These two passages remind us that such words as "seem" or "appear" have different uses in different contexts.

Thus, Descartes' expression, "It seems to me that I see light," when uttered on any ordinary occasion, might be taken to be performing one or the other of two quite different functions. (1) The expression might be used simply to report one's belief; in such a case, "It seems to me that I see light" could be replaced by "I believe that I see light." Taken in this way, the "seems" statement expresses what is directly evident, but since it is equivalent to a belief-statement, it does not add anything to the cases we have already considered. (2) "It seems to me" —or better, "It seems to *me*"—may be used not only to report a belief, but also to provide the speaker with a way out, a kind of hedge, in case the statement prefixed by "It seems to me" should turn out to be false. This function of "It seems" is thus the contrary of the performative use of "I know" to which J. L. Austin has called attention. In saying "I know," I give my hearers a kind of guarantee and, as Austin says, stake my reputation; but in saying "It seems to *me,*" I play it safe, indicating to them that what I say carries no guarantee at all and that if they choose to believe what I say they do so entirely at their own risk.[16] "It seems to me," used in this way, cannot be said to describe what is directly evident, for it cannot be said to describe anything at all.

But the word "appear" as it is used in the translation from St. Augustine—"This appears white to me"—performs still another function. (3) It may be used to describe a certain state of affairs which is not itself a belief. When "appear" is used in this descriptive, "phenomenological" way, one may say consistently and without any incongruity, "That thing appears white to me in this light, but I know that it is really gray." One may also say, again, consistently and without any incongruity, "It appears white to me in this light and I know that, as a matter of fact, it *is* white."

15 *Against the Academicians* (*Contra Academicos*), ed. and trans. Sister Mary Patricia Garvey (Milwaukee: Marquette University Press, 1942), para. 26, p. 68 of translation.

16 Austin discussed this use of "seems" in considerable detail in his posthumous *Sense and Sensibilia* (Oxford: The Clarendon Press, 1962). Compare the essay "Other Minds" in Austin's *Philosophical Papers* (Oxford: The Clarendon Press, 1961), pp. 44–84.

The latter statement illustrates two points overlooked by many contemporary philosophers. The first is that in such a statement, "appear" cannot have the hedging use just referred to, for if it did, the statement would be incongruous (which it is not); the second part of the statement ("I know that it is white") would provide a guarantee which the first part ("This appears white") withholds. The second point is that the descriptive, phenomenological use of "appears" is not restricted to the description of *illusory experiences.*

The following translation from Sextus Empiricus reminds us that "seems," as well as a number of other verbs, has this descriptive, phenomenological use:

> The same water which feels very hot when poured on inflamed spots seems lukewarm to us. And the same air seems chilly to the old but mild to those in their prime, and similarly the same sound seems to the former faint, but to the latter clearly audible. The same wine which seems sour to those who have previously eaten dates or figs seems sweet to those who have just consumed nuts or chickpeas; and the vestibule of the bathhouse which warms those entering from the outside chills those coming out.[17]

Sextus is here using certain appear-words to indicate a fact about our experience that is familiar to us all—namely, the fact that by varying the state of the subject or perceiver, or of the intervening medium, or of other conditions of observation, we may also vary the ways in which the objects that the subject perceives will appear to him. Sextus' appear-statements are simply descriptive of experience.

Some of these descriptive "appear" and "seem" statements may describe what is self-presenting, and when they do, what they express is directly evident. We can single out such a class of directly evident "appear" statements by referring to what Aristotle called the "proper objects" of the various senses and to what he called the "common sensibles."[18] The "proper objects" may be illustrated by the following: visual characteristics such as blue, green, yellow, red, white, black; auditory characteristics such as sounding or making a noise; somesthetic characteristics such as rough, smooth, hard, soft, heavy, light, hot, cold; gustatory characteristics such as sweet, sour, salt, bitter; and olfactory characteristics, such as fragrant, spicy, putrid, burned. The "common sensibles" are those characteristics such as movement, rest, number, figure, and magnitude, which, as Aristotle says, "are not peculiar to any one sense, but are common to all."

If for any such characteristic *F,* I can justify a claim to knowledge

[17] *Outlines of Pyrrhonism,* Book I, Chapter 14; abridged from Vol. I of *Sextus Empiricus,* The Loeb Classical Library, pp. 55, 63, 65. Cf. K. Lykos, "Aristotle and Plato on 'Appearing,'" *Mind,* LXXIII (1964), 496–514.

[18] See Aristotle's *De Anima,* Book II, Chapters 6 and 7.

by saying of something that it *appears F* (by saying of the wine that it now *looks* red, or *tastes* sour, to me), where the verb is intended in the descriptive, phenomenological sense just indicated, then the *appearing* in question is self-presenting and my statement expresses what is directly evident. The claim that I thus justify, by saying of something that it appears *F,* may be the claim that the thing *is F,* but as we have seen, it may also be some other claim. To the question "What justification do I have for thinking I know, or for counting it as evident, that something now *looks* red to me, or *tastes* sour?" I could reply only by reiterating that something does now look red or taste sour.[19]

Strictly speaking, "The *wine* tastes sour to me" and "*Something* looks red to me" do not express what is directly evident in our sense of this term. For the first statement implies that I am tasting *wine* and the second that there *is* a certain thing that is appearing red to me, and "I am tasting wine" and "There is a certain thing that is appearing red to me" do not express what is directly evident. What justifies me in counting it as evident that I am tasting wine is *not* simply the fact that I am tasting wine, and what justifies me in counting it as evident that a certain thing is appearing red to me (and that I am not, say, merely suffering from a hallucination) is not simply the fact that a certain thing *is* appearing red to me. To arrive at what is directly evident in these cases, we must remove the reference to wine in "The wine tastes sour to me" and we must remove the reference to the appearing thing in "That thing appears red to me." This, however, is very difficult to do, since our language was not developed for any such philosophical purpose.

Many philosophers and psychologists would turn verbs into substantives, saying in the one case, "I have a sour taste," and in the other, "I am experiencing a red appearance." Such a procedure has the advantage of enabling us to assimilate these seemings and appearings to other types of sensuous experience—to feelings, imagery, and the sensuous content of dreams and hallucinations, all of which may be "self-presenting" in the sense we have described. But in introducing the substantive "appearance," we may seem to be multiplying entities beyond necessity; for now we seem to be saying that *appearances,* as well as fences and houses, may be counted among the entities that are red. "I have a sour taste" may suggest, similarily, that *tastes,* like wine and fruit, are among the entities that may be sour. It is clear that we must proceed with great care if we are to employ this substantival terminology.[20]

[19] Or if the directly evident is to be viewed in analogy with the prime mover unmoved instead of with the prime mover that moves itself, I could say (1) that it "makes no sense" to say "It is evident to me that something now looks red or tastes sour" and (2) that "Something now looks red" or "Something now tastes sour" may yet formulate my *evidence* for something else.

[20] One of the first philosophers to note the pitfalls which this substantival, or

Let us consider another way of describing these self-presenting states. In our examples, "appear" requires a grammatical subject and thus requires a term that purports to refer not merely to a way of appearing, but also to a thing that is said to appear in that way. We may eliminate the reference to the thing that appears, however, if we *convert* our appear-sentences. Instead of saying "Something appears white to me," we may say, more awkwardly, "I am appeared white to by something." We may then eliminate the substantival "something" merely by dropping the final phrase and saying, "I am appeared white to."[21] The verbs "tastes" and "sounds" do not allow a similar conversion of "This tastes sour" and "That sounds loud," but "is appeared to" could replace such verbs: We could say "I am appeared loud to" and "I am appeared sour to," just as we have said "I am appeared white to." The words "loud," "sour," and "white," in these sentences, do not function as adjectives; the sentences do not say, of any entity, that that entity *is* loud, sour, or white. The words are used here to describe *ways* of appearing, or of being appeared to, just as "swift" and "slow" may be used to describe ways of running. They function as adverbs and our sentences would be more correct, therefore, if they were put as "I am appeared sourly to," "I am appeared whitely to," and "I am appeared loudly to."

The awkwardness of the "appears to" terminology could be avoided if, at this point, we were to introduce another verb, say, "sense," using it in a technical way as a synonym for "is appeared to." In such a case, we would say "I sense sourly," "I sense whitely," and "I sense loudly." But even this procedure will introduce ambiguities, as "I sense loudly" may suggest.

Once these terminological difficulties have been removed, is there ground for doubt concerning the directly evident character of what is expressed by statements about appearing? Doubts have been raised in recent years and we should consider these briefly.

### 10. SOME MISCONCEPTIONS

There are *some* descriptive appear-statements that do not express what is directly evident—for example, "He looks just the way his uncle did fifteen years ago." If we describe a way of appearing by *comparing* it with the

"sense datum," terminology involves was Thomas Reid; see his *Inquiry into the Human Mind* (1764), Chapter 6, sec. 20, and *Essays on the Intellectual Powers* (1785), Essay II, Chapter 16. Cf. H. A. Prichard, *Kant's Theory of Knowledge* (Oxford: The Clarendon Press, 1909), and "Appearances and Reality," *Mind* (1906); the latter is reprinted in *Realism and the Background of Phenomenology,* ed. Roderick M. Chisholm (New York: Free Press of Glencoe, Inc., 1960).

[21] But the substantive "I" remains. Recall the beginning of our quotation from Leibniz: "Our direct awareness of our own existence and of our thoughts provides us with the primary truths *a posteriori*. . . ."

way in which some physical thing happens to have appeared in the past, or with the way in which some physical thing is thought normally to appear, then the justification for what we say about the way of appearing will depend in part upon the justification for what we say about the physical thing; and what we say about the physical thing will not now be directly evident. Now it has been argued that the types of appear-statements we have just been considering *also* involve some comparison with previously experienced objects, and hence, that what they express cannot ever be said to be directly evident. It has been suggested, for example, that if I say, "This appears white," then I am making a "comparison between a present object and a formerly seen object."[22] What justification is there for saying this?

It is true that the expression "appears white" may be used to abbreviate "appears the way in which white things normally appear." But this should not prevent us from seeing that things may also be the other way around: "white thing" can be used to abbreviate "thing having the color of things that normally appear white." In such a case, the expression, "appear white," as it is used in the latter sentence, is *not* used to abbreviate "appear the way in which white things normally appear." For in saying that "white thing" may be used to abbreviate "thing having the color of things that normally appear white," we are *not* saying simply that "white thing" may be used to abbreviate "thing having the color of things which ordinarily appear the way in which *white things* normally appear." Therefore, when we say that "white thing" may be used to abbreviate "thing having the color of things that ordinarily appear white," the point of "appear white" is not to compare a way of appearing with anything. In this use of "appear white," we may say significantly and without redundancy, "Things that *are* white normally *appear* white." And this is the way in which we should interpret "This appears white to me" in the quotation above from St. Augustine. More generally, it is in terms of this descriptive, noncomparative use of our other "appear" and "seem" words (including "looks," "tastes," "sounds," and the like) that we are to interpret those appear-statements that are said to be directly evident.

But philosophers have offered three different arguments to show that appear-words cannot be used in this noncomparative way. Each of the three arguments, I believe, is quite obviously invalid.

1. The first argument may be summarized in this way: "(a) Sentences such as 'This appears white' are 'parasitical upon' sentences such as 'This *is* white'; that is to say, in order to understand 'This appears white,' one must *first* be able to understand 'This is white.' Therefore (b) 'This

22 Hans Reichenbach, *Experience and Prediction* (Chicago: University of Chicago Press, 1938), p. 176.

appears white' ordinarily means the same as 'This appears in the way in which white things ordinarily appear.' Hence (c) 'This is white' *cannot* be used to mean the same as 'This is the sort of thing that ordinarily appears white,' where 'appears white' is used in the way you have just described. And so (d) then there is no clear sense in which what is expressed by 'This appears white' can be said to be directly evident."

There is an advantage in thus making the argument explicit. For to see what the conclusion (d) does not follow from the premise (a), we have only to note that (c) does not follow from (b). From the fact that a linguistic expression is ordinarily used in one way, it does not follow that that expression may not also sometimes be used in another way. And so even if the linguistic hypothesis upon which the argument is based were true, the conclusion does not follow from the premise.

2. It has also been argued: "(a) If the sentence 'I am appeared white to' does not express a comparison between a present way of appearing and anything else, then the sentence is completely empty and says nothing at all about a present way of appearing. But (b) if 'I am appeared white to' expresses what is directly evident, then it cannot assert a comparison between a present way of appearing and anything else. Therefore, (c) either 'I am appeared white to' is empty or it does not express what is directly evident."

Here the difficulty lies in the first premise. It may well be true that if an appear-sentence is to be used to communicate anything to another person, it must assert some comparison of things. Thus if I wish *you* to know the way in which I am appeared to now, I must relate this way of being appeared to with something that is familiar to you. ("Describe the taste? It's something like the taste of a mango.") But our question is not: "If you are to understand me when I say something about the way in which I am appeared to, must I be comparing that way of appearing with the way in which some object, familiar to you, happens to appear?" The question is, more simply: "Can I apprehend the way in which I am now appeared to without thereby supposing, with respect to some object, that the way I am being appeared to is the way in which that object sometimes appears or has sometimes appeared?" From the fact that the first of these two questions must be answered in the negative, it does not follow that the second must also be answered in the negative.

The argument, moreover, presupposes an absurd thesis about the nature of thought or predication. This thesis might be expressed by saying that "all judgments are comparative." To see that this is absurd, we have only to consider more carefully what it says. It tells us that in order to assert or to believe, with respect to any particular thing $x$, that $x$ has a certain property $F$, one must *compare* $x$ with some other thing $y$ and thus assert or believe of $x$ that it has something in common with the other thing *y*. But clearly, we cannot derive "*x* is *F*" from "*x* resembles *y*" unless, among other things, we can say or believe *noncomparatively* that *y* is *F*.

3. The final argument designed to show that appear-statements cannot express what is directly evident, may be put as follows: "(a) In saying 'Something appears white,' you are making certain assumptions about language; you are assuming, for example, that the word 'white,' or the phrase 'appears white,' is being used in the way in which you have used it on other occasions, or in the way in which other people have used it. Therefore (b) when you say 'This appears white,' you are saying something not only about your present experience, but also about all of these other occasions. But (c) what you are saying about these other occasions is not directly evident. And therefore (d) 'This is white' does not express what is directly evident."

The false step in this argument is the inference from (a) to (b). We must distinguish the belief that a speaker has about the words that he is using from the belief that he is using those words to express. What holds true for the former need not hold true for the latter. A Frenchman, believing that "potatoes" is English for apples, may use, "There are potatoes in the basket" to express the belief that there are apples in the basket; from the fact that he has a mistaken belief about "potatoes" and "apples," it does not follow that he has a mistaken belief about potatoes and apples. Similarly, it may be that what a man believes about his own use of the expression "appears white" is something that is not directly evident to him—indeed what he believes about his own language may even be false and unreasonable; but from these facts it does not follow that what he intends to assert when he utters "This appears white to me" is something that cannot be directly evident.[23]

We have, then, singled out various types of statements expressing what is directly evident. Most of these statements, as Leibniz said, refer to our *thoughts;* they may say what we are thinking, believing, hoping, fearing, wishing, wondering, desiring, loving, hating; or they may say what we think we know, or think we are remembering, or think we are perceiving. Some of them will refer to our *actions,* at least to the extent of saying what we are trying or undertaking to do at any particular time. And some of them will refer to ways in which we *sense,* or are *appeared* to.

[23] For a further defense of this way of looking at appearing, compare John Pollock, *Knowledge and Justification* (Princeton: Princeton University Press, 1974), pp. 71–79.

CHAPTER THREE

# The Truths of Reason

There are also two kinds of truths: those of reasoning and those of fact. The truths of reasoning are necessary, and their opposite is impossible. Those of fact, however, are contingent, and their opposite is possible. When a truth is necessary, we can find the reason by analysis, resolving the truth into simpler ideas and simpler truths until we reach those that are primary.

LEIBNIZ, *Monadology* 33

## 1. A TRADITIONAL METAPHYSICAL VIEW

Reason, according to one traditional view, functions as a source of knowledge. This view, when it is clearly articulated, may be seen to involve a number of metaphysical presuppositions and it is, therefore, unacceptable to many contemporary philosophers. But the alternatives to this view, once *they* are clearly articulated, may be seen to be at least problematic and to imply an extreme form of skepticism.

According to this traditional view, there are certain *truths of reason* and some of these truths of reason can be known *a priori*. These truths pertain to certain abstract or eternal objects—things such as properties, numbers, and propositions or states of affairs, things that would exist even if there weren't any contingent things such as persons and physical objects. To present the traditional view, we will first illustrate such truths and then we will try to explain what is meant by saying that we know some of these truths *a priori*.

Some of the truths of reason concern what we might call relations of "inclusion" and "exclusion" that obtain among various properties. The relation of *inclusion* among properties is illustrated by these facts: The property of being square includes that of being rectangular, and that of being red includes that of being colored. The relation of *exclusion* is exemplified by these facts: The property of being square excludes that of being circular, and that of being red excludes that of being blue. To say that one property excludes another, therefore, is to say more than that the one fails to include the other. Being red fails to include being heavy, but it does not exclude being heavy; if it excluded being heavy, as it excludes being blue, then nothing could be both red and heavy.[1]

Other examples of such inclusion and exclusion are these: Being both red and square includes being red and excludes being circular; being both red and warm-if-red includes being warm; being both nonwarm and warm-if-red excludes being red.

These relations are all such that they hold *necessarily.* And they would hold, therefore, even if there weren't any contingent things.

One can formulate more general truths about the relations of inclusion and exclusion. For example, every property *F* and every property *G* is such that *F*'s excluding *G* includes *G*'s excluding *F; F*'s excluding *G* includes *F*'s including not-*G; F* excludes non-*F,* and includes *F*-or-*G*. And such truths as these are necessary.

States of affairs or propositions are analogous to properties.[2] Like properties, they are related by inclusion and exclusion; for example, "some men being Greeks" includes, and is included by, "some Greeks being men," and excludes "no Greeks being men." States of affairs, like properties, may be compound; for example, "some men being Greek and Plato being Roman"; "Socrates being wise or Xantippe being wise." The conjunctive state of affairs, "Socrates being a man and all men being mortal," includes "Socrates being mortal" and excludes "no men being mortal." Such truths about states of affairs are examples of truths of logic. And such truths, according to the traditional doctrine, are all necessary. They would hold even if there had been no Socrates or Greeks or men.

Other truths of reason are those of mathematics; for example, the truths expressed by "2 and 3 are 5" and "7 and 5 are 12."

1 "Being red excludes being blue" should not be taken to rule out the possibility of a thing being red in one part and blue in another; it tells us only that being red in one part at one time excludes being blue in exactly that same part at exactly that same time. The point might be put even more exactly by saying that it is necesarily true that anything that is red has a part that is not blue.

2 For the present, I will use "state of affairs" and "proposition" more or less interchangeably. Whenever we say of a state of affairs that it "occurs" or "obtains," we could say, instead, of a proposition that it is "true"; and conversely. The relation between these concepts will be discussed in Chapter 5.

**2. NOT ALL KNOWLEDGE OF NECESSITY IS *A POSTERIORI***

When it is said that these truths of reason are known (or are capable of being known) "*a priori*," what is meant may be suggested by contrasting them with what is known "*a posteriori*." A single example may suggest what is intended when it is said that these truths may be known without being known *a posteriori*.

Corresponding to "Being red excludes being blue," which is a truth about properties, the following general statement is a truth about individual things: "Necessarily, every individual thing, past, present, or future, is such that if it is red then it is not blue." If the latter truth were known *a posteriori*, then it would be justified by some induction or inductions; our evidence presumably would consist in the fact that a great variety of red things and a great variety of nonblue things have been observed in the past, and that up to now, no red things have been blue. We might thus inductively confirm "Every individual thing, past, present, or future, is such that if it is red then it is not blue." Reflecting upon this conclusion, we may then go on to make still another step. We will proceed to the further conclusion, "Being red excludes being blue," and then deduce, "Necessarily, every individual thing, past, present, or future, is such that if it is red then it is not blue."

Thus, there might be said to be three steps involved in an inductive justification of "Necessarily, being red excludes being blue": (1) the accumulation of instances—"This red thing is not blue," "That blue thing is not red," and so on—along with the summary statement, "No red thing observed up to now has been blue"; (2) the inductive inference from these data to "Every individual thing, past, present, and future, is such that if it is red then it is not blue"; (3) the step from this inductive conclusion to "Being red excludes being blue," or "Necessarily, every individual thing, past, present, or future, is such that if it is red then it is not blue."

Why *not* say that such "truths of reason" are thus known *a posteriori?* For one thing, some of these truths pertain to properties that have never been exemplified. If we take "square," "rectangular," and "circular" in the precise way in which these words are usually interpreted in geometry, we must say that nothing is square, rectangular, or circular; things in nature, as Plato said, "fall short" of having such properties.[3] Hence, to justify "Necessarily, being square includes being rectangular and excludes being circular," we cannot even take the first of the three steps illustrated above; there being no squares, we cannot collect instances of squares that are rectangles and squares that are not circles.

3 *Phaedo,* 75a.

For another thing, application of induction would seem to presuppose a knowledge of the "truths of reason." In setting out to confirm an inductive hypothesis, we must be able to recognize what its consequences would be. Ordinarily, to recognize these we must apply deduction; we take the hypothesis along with other things that we know and we see what is then implied. All of this, it would seem, involves apprehension of truths of reason—such truths as may be suggested by "For all states of affairs, $p$ and $q$, the conjunctive state of affairs, composed of $p$ and of either not-$p$ or $q$, includes $q$," and "All *A*'s being *B* excludes some *A*'s not being *B*." Hence, even if we are able to justify some of the "truths of reason" by inductive procedures, any such justification will presuppose others, and we will be left with some "truths of reason" which we have not justified by means of induction.[4]

And finally, the last of the three steps described above—the step from the inductive generalization "Every individual thing, past, present, and future, is such that if it is red then it is not blue" to "Being red excludes being blue," or "Necessarily, every individual thing, past, present, and future, is such that if it is red then it is not blue"—remains obscure.

How do we reach this final step? What justifies us in saying that *necessarily*, every individual thing, past, present, and future, is such that if it is red then it is not blue? The English philosopher, William Whewell, wrote that the mere accumulation of instances cannot afford the slightest ground for the necessity of a generalization upon those instances. "Experience," he said, "can observe and record what has happened; but she cannot find, in any case, or in any accumulation of cases, any reason for what *must* happen. She may see objects side by side, but she cannot see a reason why they must ever be side by side. She finds certain events to occur in succession; but the succession supplies, in its occurrence, no reasons for its recurrence; she contemplates external objects; but she cannot detect any internal bond, which indissolubly connects the future with the past, the possible with the real. To learn a proposition by experience, and to see it to be necessarily true, are two altogether different processes of thought. . . . If anyone does not clearly comprehend this distinction of necessary and contingent truths, he will not be able to go along with us in our researches into the foundations of human knowledge; nor indeed, to pursue with success any speculation on the subject."[5]

[4] Cf. Gottlob Frege, *The Foundations of Arithmetic* (Oxford: Basil Blackwell, 1950), pp. 16–17; first published in 1884.

[5] William Whewell, *Philosophy of the Inductive Sciences Founded upon Their History, I* (London: J. W. Parker & Son, 1840), pp. 59–61.

**3. INTUITIVE INDUCTION**

Plato suggested that in order to acquire a knowledge of necessity, we should turn away from "the twilight of becoming and perishing" and contemplate the world of "the absolute and eternal and immutable."[6] According to Aristotle, however, and to subsequent philosophers in the tradition with which we are here concerned, one way of obtaining the requisite intuition is to consider the particular things of this world.

As a result of perceiving a particular blue thing, or a number of particular blue things, we may come to know what it is for a thing to be blue, and thus, we may be said to know what the property of being blue is. And as a result of perceiving a particular red thing, or a number of particular red things, we may come to know what it is for a thing to be red, and thus, to know what the property of being red is. Then, having this knowledge of what it is to be red and of what it is to be blue, we are able to see that being red excludes being blue, and that this is necessarily so.

Thus, Aristotle tells us that as a result of perceiving Callias and a number of other particular men, we come to see what it is for a thing to have the property of being human. And then, by considering the property of being human, we come to see that being human includes being animal, and that this is necessarily so.[7]

Looking to these examples, we may distinguish four stages:

1. There is the perception of the individual things—in the one case, the perception of the particular red things and blue things, and in the other, the perception of Callias and the other particular men.

2. There is a process of abstraction—we come to see what it is for a thing to be red and for a thing to be blue, and we come to see what it is for a thing to be a man.

3. There is the intuitive apprehension of certain relations holding between properties—in the one case, apprehension of the fact that being red excludes being blue, and in the other, apprehension of the fact that being rational and animal includes being animal.

4. Once we have acquired this intuitive knowledge, then, *ipso facto,* we also know the truth of reason expressed by "Necessarily, everything is such that if it is red then it is not blue" and "Necessarily, everything is such that if it is human then it is animal."

Aristotle called this process "induction." But since it differs in essential respects from what subsequently came to be known as "induction," some other term, say, "intuitive induction," may be less misleading.[8]

[6] *Republic,* 479, 508.

[7] *Posterior Analytics,* 100a–100b.

[8] This term was proposed by W. E. Johnson, *Logic* (London: Cambridge University

If we have performed an "intuitive induction" in the manner described, then we may say that by contemplating the relation between properties we are able to know that being red excludes being blue and thus to know that *necessarily*, everything is such that if it is red then it is not blue. And we can say, therefore, that the universal generalization, as well as the proposition about properties, is known *a priori*. The order of justification thus differs from that of the enumerative induction considered earlier, where one attempts to justify the statement about properties by reference to a generalization about particular things.

There is a superficial resemblance between "intuitive induction" and "induction by simple enumeration," since in each case, we start with particular instances and then proceed beyond them. Thus, when we make an induction by enumeration, we may proceed from "This *A* is *B*," "That *A* is *B*," and so on, to "In all probability, all *A*'s are *B*'s," or to "In all probability, the next *A* is *B*." But in an induction by enumeration, the function of the particular instances is to *justify* the conclusion. If we find subsequently that our perceptions of the particular instances were unveridical, say, that the things we took to be *A*'s were not *A*'s at all, then the inductive argument would lose whatever force it may have had. In an "intuitive induction," however, the particular perceptions are only incidental to the conclusion. This may be seen in the following way.

Let us suppose that the knowledge expressed by the two sentences "Necessarily, being red excludes being blue" and "Necessarily, being human includes being animal" is arrived at by intuitive induction; and let us suppose further that in each case, the process began with the perception of certain particular things. Neither conclusion depends for its *justification* upon the particular perceptions which led to the knowledge concerned. As Duns Scotus put it, the perception of the particular things is only the "occasion" of acquiring the knowledge. If we happen to find our perception was unveridical, this finding will have no bearing upon the result. "If the senses from which these terms were received were all false, or what is more deceptive, if some were false and others true, I still maintain that the intellect would not be deceived about such principles. . . ."[9] If what we take to be Callias is not a man at all, but only a clever imitation of a man, then, if the imitation is clever enough, our deceptive experience will still be an occasion for contemplating the

---

Press, 1921), Part II, pp. 191ff. Aristotle uses the term "induction" in the passages cited in the *Posterior Analytics;* cf. *The Nicomachean Ethics,* Book VI, Chapter 3, 1139b. Compare Franz Brentano, *The Origin of Our Knowledge of Right and Wrong* (London: Routledge and Kegan Paul, 1969), pp. 111–113.

[9] *Philosophical Writings,* ed. and trans. Alan Wolter (New York: Thomas Nelson & Sons, 1962), p. 109 (the Nelson philosophical texts); cf. p. 103.

property of being human—the property of being both rational and animal—and thus, for coming to know that being human includes being animal.

Leibniz thus observes: ". . . if I should discover any demonstrative truth, mathematical or other, while dreaming (as might in fact be), it would be just as certain as if I had been awake. This shows us how intelligible truth is independent of the truth of the existence outside of us of sensible and material things."[10]

It may be, indeed, that to perform an intuitive induction—i.e., to "abstract" a certain property, contemplate it, and then see what it includes and excludes—we need only to *think* of some individual thing as having that property. By thinking about a blue thing and a red thing, for example, we may come to see that being blue excludes being red. Thus, Ernst Mach spoke of "experiments in the imagination."[11] And E. Husserl, whose language may have been needlessly Platonic, said, "The Eidos, the *pure essence,* can be exemplified intuitively in the data of experience, data of perception, memory, and so forth, but just as readily *also in the mere data of fancy. . . .*"[12]

According to this traditional account, then, once we have acquired some concepts (once we know, with respect to certain attributes, just *what* it is for something to have those attributes), we will also be in a position to know just *what* it is for a proposition or state of affairs to be necessary—to be necessarily such that it is true or necessarily such that it obtains. Then, by contemplating or reflecting upon certain propositions or states of affairs, we will be able to see that *they* are necessary.

This kind of knowledge has traditionally been called *a priori.*

## 4. AXIOMS

Speaking very roughly, we might say that one mark of an *a priori* proposition is this: once you understand it, you see that it is true. We might call this the traditional conception of the *a priori.* Thus Leibniz remarks: "You will find in a hundred places that the Scholastics have said that these propositions are evident, *ex terminis,* as soon as the terms are understood. . . ."[13]

10 *The Philosophical Works of Leibniz,* ed. G. M. Duncan (New Haven: The Tuttle, Morehouse & Taylor Co., 1908), p. 161.

11 *Erkenntnis und Irrtum* (Leipzig: Felix Meiner, 1905), pp. 180ff.

12 E. Husserl, *Ideas: General Introduction to Phenomenology* (New York: The Macmillan Company, 1931), p. 57.

13 G. W. Leibniz, *New Essays Concerning Human Understanding,* Book IV, Chapter 7 (Open Court edition), p. 462. Compare Alice Ambrose and Morris Lazerowitz, *Fundamentals of Symbolic Logic* (New York: Holt, Rinehart and Winston, Inc., 1962): "A proposition is said to be true *a priori* if its truth can be ascertained by examination of the proposition alone or if it is deducible from propositions whose truth is so

If we say an *a priori* proposition is one such that "once you understand it then you see that it is true," we must take the term "understand" in a somewhat rigid sense. You couldn't be said to "understand" a proposition, in the sense intended, unless you can grasp *what* it is for that proposition to be true. The properties or attributes that the proposition implies—those that would be instantiated if the proposition were true—must be properties or attributes that you can grasp in the sense that we have tried to explicate. To "understand" a proposition, in the sense intended, then, it is not enough merely to be able to say what *sentence* in your language happens to express that proposition. The proposition must be one that you have contemplated and reflected upon.

One cannot *accept* a proposition, in the sense in which we have been using the word "accept," unless one also *understands* that proposition. We might say, therefore, that an *a priori* proposition is one such that, if you accept it, then it becomes certain for you. (For if you accept it, then you understand it, and as soon as you understand it, it becomes certain for you.) This account of the *a priori,* however, would be somewhat broad. We know some *a priori* propositions on the basis of others and these propositions are not themselves such that, once they are understood, then they are certain.

But let us begin by trying to characterize more precisely those *a priori* propositions which are not known on the basis of any *other* propositions.

Leibniz said that these propositions are the "first lights." He wrote: "The immediate apperception of our existence and of our thoughts furnishes us with the first truths *a posteriori,* or of fact, i.e., the *first experiences,* as the identical propositions contain the first truths *a priori,* or of reason, i.e., the *first lights.* Both are incapable of proof, and may be called *immediate. . . .*"[14]

The traditional term for those *a priori* propositions which are "incapable of proof" is *axiom.* Thus Frege wrote: "Since the time of antiquity an axiom has been taken to be a thought whose truth is known without being susceptible to demonstration by a logical chain of reasoning."[15] In *one* sense, of course, every true proposition *h* is capable of proof, for there will always be other true propositions from which we can derive *h* by means of some principle of logic. What did Leibniz and Frege mean, then, when they said that an axiom is "incapable of proof"?

The answer is suggested by Aristotle. An axiom, or "basic truth," he

---

ascertained, and by examination of nothing else. . . . Understanding the words used in expressing these propositions is sufficient for determining that they are true." P. 17.

14 *New Essays Concerning Human Understanding,* Book IV, Chapter 9, p. 499.

15 Gottlob Frege, *Kleine Schriften* (Hildesheim: Georg Olms Verlagsbuchhandlung, 1967), p. 262.

said, is a proposition "which has no other proposition prior to it"; there is no proposition which is "better known" than it is.[16] We could say that if one proposition is "better known" than another, then accepting the one proposition is more reasonable than accepting the other. Hence, if an axiomatic proposition is one such that no other proposition is better known than it is, then it is one that is certain. (It will be recalled that we characterized *certainty* in Chapter 1. We there said that a proposition *h* is *certain* for a person *S*, provided that *h* is evident for *S* and provided that there is no other proposition *i* which is such that it is *more* reasonable for *S* to accept *i* than it is for him to accept *h*.) Hence Aristotle said that an axiom is a "primary premise." Its ground does not lie in the fact that it is seen to follow from *other* propositions. Therefore we cannot prove such a proposition by making use of any premises that are "better known" than it is. (By "a proof," then, Aristotle, Leibniz, and Frege meant more than "a valid derivation from premises that are true.")

Let us now try to say what it is for a proposition or state of affairs to be an *axiom:*

D3.1 *h* is an *axiom* =Df *h* is necessarily such that (i) it is true and (ii) for every *S*, if *S* accepts *h*, then *h* is certain for *S*.

The following propositions among countless others may be said to be axioms in our present sense of the term:

If some men are Greeks, then some Greeks are men.
If Jones is ill and Smith is away, then Jones is ill.
The sum of 5 and 3 is 8.
The product of 4 and 2 is 8.

For most of us, i.e., for those of us who really *do* consider them, they may be said to be *axiomatic* in the following sense:

D3.2 *h* is *axiomatic* for *S* =Df (i) *h* is an axiom and (ii) *S* accepts *h*.

We may assume that any conjunction of axioms is itself an axiom. But it does not follow from this assumption that any conjunction of propositions which are axiomatic for a subject *S* is itself axiomatic for *S*. If two propositions are axiomatic for *S* and if *S* does not accept their conjunction, then the conjunction is not axiomatic for *S*. (Failure to accept their conjunction need not be a sign that *S* is unreasonable. It may be a sign merely that the conjunction is too complex an object for *S* to grasp.)

We have suggested that our knowledge of what is axiomatic is a subspecies of our *a priori* knowledge, that is to say, some of the things we

[16] *Posterior Analytics,* Book I, Chapter 2.

know *a priori* are *not* axiomatic in the present sense. They are *a priori* but they are not what Aristotle called "primary premises."

What would be an example of a proposition that is *a priori* for *S* but not axiomatic for *S*? Consider the last two axioms on our list above; i.e.,

The sum of 5 and 3 is 8.
The product of 4 and 2 is 8.

Let us suppose that their conjunction is also an axiom and that *S* accepts this conjunction; therefore the conjunction is axiomatic for *S*. Let us suppose further that the following proposition is axiomatic for *S:*

If the sum of 5 and 3 is 8 and the product of 4 and 2 is 8, then the sum of 5 and 3 is the product of 4 and 2.

We will say that, if, in such a case, *S* accepts the proposition

The sum of 5 and 3 is the product of 4 and 2

then that proposition is *a priori* for *S*. Yet the proposition may not be one which is such that it is certain for anyone who accepts it. It may be that one can consider *that* proposition without thereby seeing that it is true.

There are various ways in which we might now attempt to characterize this broader concept of the *a priori*. Thus we might say: "You know a proposition *a priori* provided you accept it and it is implied by propositions that are axiomatic for you." But this would imply that *any* necessary proposition that you happen to accept is one that you know *a priori* to be true. (Any necessary proposition *h* is implied by any axiomatic proposition *e*. Indeed any necessary proposition *h* is implied by *any* proposition *e*—whether or not *e* is axiomatic and whether or not *e* is true or false. For if *h* is necessary, then, it is necessarily true that, for any proposition *e,* either *e* is false or *h* is true. And to say "*e* implies *h*" is to say it is necessarily true that either *e* is false or *h* is true.) *Some* of the necessary propositions that we accept may *not* be propositions that we know *a priori*. They may be such that, if we know them, we know them *a posteriori*—on the basis of authority. Or they may be such that we cannot be said to know them at all.

To capture the broader concept of the *a priori,* we might say that a proposition is known *a priori* provided it is axiomatic that the proposition follows from something that is axiomatic. But let us say, more carefully:

D3.3 *h* is known *a priori* by *S* =Df There is an *e* such that (i) *e* is axiomatic for *S,* (ii) the proposition, *e* implies *h,* is axiomatic for *S,* and (iii) *S* accepts *h.*

We may add that a person knows a proposition *a posteriori* if he knows the proposition but doesn't know it *a priori*.[17]

We may assume that what is thus known *a priori* is evident. But the *a priori*, unlike the axiomatic, need not be certain. This accords with St. Thomas's observation that "those who have knowledge of the principles [i.e. the axioms] have a more certain knowledge than the knowledge which is through demonstration."[18]

But is this account too restrictive? What if *S* derives a proposition from a set of axioms, not by means of one or two simple steps, but as a result of a complex proof, involving a series of interrelated steps? If the proof is formally valid, then shouldn't we say that *S* knows the proposition *a priori?*

I think that the answer is no. Complex proofs or demonstrations, as John Locke pointed out, have a certain limitation. They take time. The result is that the "evident lustre" of the early steps may be lost by the time we reach the conclusion: "In long deductions, and the use of many proofs, the memory does not always so readily retain." Therefore, he said, demonstrative knowledge "is more imperfect than intuitive knowledge."[19] Descartes also noted that memory is essential to demonstrative knowledge. He remarks in *Rules for the Direction of the Mind* that, if we can *remember* having deduced a certain conclusion step by step from a set of premises that are "known by intuition," then, even though we may not now recall each of the particular steps, we are justified in saying that the conclusion is "known by deduction."[20] But if, in the course of a demonstration, we must rely upon memory at various stages, thus using as premises contingent propositions about what we happen to remember, then, although we might be said to have "demonstrative knowledge" of our conclusion, in a somewhat broad sense of the expression "demonstrative knowledge," we cannot be said to have an *a priori* demonstration of the conclusion.

[17] It should be noted that philosophers have used "*a priori*" and "*a posteriori*" in several different ways; it is not to be assumed that the present definitions are compatible with every such use. Compare David Benfield, "The *A Priori—A Posteriori* Distinction," *Philosophy and Phenomenological Research,* XXXV (1974), 151–166.

[18] Thomas Aquinas, *Exposition of the Posterior Analytics of Aristotle,* trans. Pierre Conway, Part II, Lecture 20, No. 4 (Quebec: M. Doyon, 1952).

[19] *Essay Concerning Human Understanding,* Book IV, Chapter 2, sec. 7.

[20] See *The Philosophical Works of Descartes,* I, E. S. Haldane and G. R. T. Ross, eds. (London: Cambridge University Press, 1934), p. 8. Some version of Descartes' principle should be an essential part of any theory of evidence. Compare Norman Malcolm's suggestion: "If a man previously had grounds for being sure that *p,* and now remembers that *p,* but does not remember what his grounds were," then he "*has* the same grounds he previously had." *Knowledge and Certainty* (Englewood Cliffs, N.J.: Prentice-Hall, Inc., 1963), p. 230.

Of course, we may make mistakes in attempting to carry out a proof, just as we may make mistakes in doing simple arithmetic. And one might well ask: How can this be, if the propositions we are concerned with are known *a priori*? Sometimes, as the quotation from Locke suggests, there has been a slip of memory. Perhaps we are mistaken about just *what* the propositions are that we proved at an earlier step—just as, in doing arithmetic, we may mistakenly think we have carried the 2, or we may pass over some figure having thought that we included it, or we may inadvertently include something twice. And there are also occasions when we may just seem to get the *a priori* proposition wrong. In my haste I say to myself, "9 and 6 are 13," and then the result will come out wrong. But when I do this, I am not really considering the proposition that 9 and 6 are 13. I may just be considering the formula, "9 and 6 are 13," which sounds right at the time, and not considering at all the proposition that that formula is used to express.

We have said what it is for a proposition to be known *a priori* by a given subject. But we should note, finally, that propositions are sometimes said to be *a priori* even though they may not be known by anyone at all. Thus Kant held that "mathematical propositions, strictly so called, are always judgments *a priori*."[21] In saying this, he did not mean to be saying merely that mathematical propositions are necessarily true; he was saying something about their epistemic status and something about the way in which they could be known. Yet he could not have been saying that all mathematical propositions are known or even believed, by someone or other, to be true; for there are propositions of mathematics that no one knows to be true; and there are propositions of mathematics that no one has ever even considered. What would it be, then, to say that a proposition might be *a priori* even though it has not been considered by anyone? I think the answer can only be that the proposition is one that *could* be known *a priori*. In other words:

D3.4 *h* is *a priori* =Df It is possible that there is someone for whom *h* is *a priori*.

This definition allows us to say that a proposition may be "objectively *a priori*"—"objectively" in that it is *a priori* whether or not anyone knows it *a priori*.

Our definitions are in the spirit of several familiar dicta concerning the *a priori*. Thus, we may say, as Kant did, that necessity is a mark of the *a priori*—provided we mean by this that if a proposition is *a priori*

[21] I. Kant, *Critique of Pure Reason*, trans. Norman Kemp Smith (London: Macmillan and Co., Ltd., 1933), p. 52.

then it is necessary.[22] For our definitions assure us that whatever is *a priori* is necessarily true.

The definitions also enable us to say, as St. Thomas did, that these propositions are "manifest through themselves."[23] For an axiomatic proposition is one such that, once it is reflected upon or considered, then it is certain. What a given person knows *a priori* may not *itself* be such that, once it is considered, it is certain. But our definition enables us to say that, if a proposition is one that is *a priori* for you, then you can see that it follows from a proposition that is axiomatic.

Kant said that our *a priori* knowledge, like all other knowledge, "begins with experience" but that, unlike our *a posteriori* knowledge, it does not "arise out of experience."[24] *A priori* knowledge may be said to "begin with experience" in the following sense. There is no *a priori* knowledge until some proposition is in fact contemplated and understood. Moreover, the acceptance of a proposition that is axiomatic is sufficient to make that proposition an axiom for whoever accepts it. But *a priori* knowledge does not "arise out of experience." For, if a proposition is axiomatic or *a priori* for us, then we have all the evidence we need to see that it is true. Understanding is enough; it is not necessary to make any further inquiry.

What Leibniz called "first truths *a posteriori*" coincide with what we have called the *directly evident*. And his "first truths *a priori*" coincide with what we have called the *axiomatic*. If we chose, we might say that both sets of truths are directly evident—in which case, our account of the directly evident in Chapter 2 could be said to be an account of what is *directly evident a posteriori*, and our account of what is axiomatic could be said to be an account of what is *directly evident a priori*.[25]

### 5. *A PRIORI* AND *A POSTERIORI*

Kant had said, as we have noted, that "necessity is a mark of the *a priori*." We may accept Kant's dictum, if we take it to mean that what is known *a priori* is necessary.

But is it possible to know a necessary proposition to be true and not

[22] Compare *Critique of Pure Reason*, B4 (Kemp Smith edition), p. 44. But we should not assume that if a proposition is necessary and known to be true, then it is *a priori*.

[23] St. Thomas Aquinas, *Exposition of the Posterior Analytics of Aristotle*, Part I, Lecture 4, No. 10, p. 26.

[24] *Critique of Pure Reason*, B1 (Kemp Smith edition), p. 41.

[25] This terminology is close to that of Franz Brentano. Compare his *The True and the Evident* (London: Routledge & Kegan Paul, 1966), pp. 130ff.

to know this *a priori?* In other words, can we know some necessary propositions *a posteriori?*

A possible example of a proposition that is known *a posteriori* and is yet necessary might be a logical theorem which one accepts on the ground that reputable logicians assert it to be true. Whether there are in fact any such propositions depends upon two things, each of them somewhat problematic.

The first is that such a proposition cannot be said to be *known* to be true unless such testimonial evidence is sufficient for knowledge. And this is a question we cannot discuss in the present book.[26]

The second is that such a proposition cannot be said to be known to be true unless it is one that the man *accepts*. But when a man, as we say, accepts a theorem on the basis of authority and not on the basis of demonstration, is it the theorem *itself* that he accepts or is it what Brentano calls a "surrogate" for the theorem?[27] If a man reads a logical text, finds there a formula which expresses a certain logical principle, and then, knowing that the author is reputable, concludes that the formula is true, it may well be that the man does *not* accept the logical principle. What he accepts is, rather, the contingent proposition to the effect that a certain formula in a book expresses a logical principle that is true.

But if we waive these difficulties, then perhaps we may say that there is an analytic *a posteriori*—or at least that some of the logical truths that we know are such that we know them only *a posteriori.*[28]

But even if some of the things we know *a posteriori* are logically true, there is at least this additional epistemic relation holding between the necessary and the *a priori:*

If a man knows—or someone once knew—*a posteriori* that a certain necessary proposition is true, then *someone* knows *a priori* that some necessary proposition is true. If the first man bases his knowledge on the testimony of authority, and if this authority in turn bases his knowledge upon the testimony of some other authority, then sooner or later there will be an "ultimate authority" who knows some proposition *a priori.*

26 On the importance of testimony for the theory of evidence, compare: James F. Ross, "Testimonial Evidence," in *Analysis and Metaphysics,* ed. Keith Lehrer (Dordrecht: D. Reidel Publishing Company, 1975), pp. 35–55; and I. M. Bochenski, *Was ist Autorität?* (Herder: Freiburg im Breisgau, 1974).

27 Cf. Franz Brentano *Grundzuge der Ästhetik* (Bern: A. Franke, 1959), p. 167.

28 And so, given Definition D3.4 above, the definition of the "objective" sense of *a priori,* we may seriously consider the possibility discussed by Bernard Bolzano: that a proposition "can be objectively *a priori* although it is subjectively only *a posteriori.*" Bernard Bolzano, *Theory of Science,* trans. Rolf George (Oxford: Basil Blackwell, 1972), p. 184.

## 6. SKEPTICISM WITH RESPECT TO THE *A PRIORI*

Let us now consider a skeptical objection to what we have been saying.

"You have said what it is for a proposition to be axiomatic for a person and you have given examples of propositions which, you say, are axiomatic for you and presumably for others. But how do you know that those propositions are axiomatic? How do you know that they satisfy the terms of your definitions?

"If you really do know that they are axiomatic, then you must have some *general principle* by means of which you can apply your definitions. There must be something about your experience that guarantees these propositions for you and you must *know* that it guarantees them. But what could the principle be?

"The most you can say, surely, is that such propositions just *seem* to be true, or that when you reflect on them you find you cannot doubt them and that you cannot help but accept them. But, as the history of science makes clear, such facts as these provide no guarantee that the propositions in question are true. Notoriously, there have been ever so many false propositions which reasonable people have found they couldn't doubt. And some of these may well have been taken as axiomatic. Consider the logical paradoxes, for example. People found they couldn't help but believe certain propositions, and as a result they became entangled in contradictions."

The objection may be summarized as follows:

1. You cannot know that a given proposition is axiomatic for you unless the proposition is one such that, when you contemplate it, you have a kind of experience—say, a strong feeling of conviction—that provides you with a guarantee that the proposition is true. But
2. there is no experience which will provide such a guarantee. Therefore
3. you cannot really know, with respect to any proposition that it is one that is axiomatic.

Is this a valid argument? The conclusion certainly follows from the premises. And, knowing the history of human error, we can hardly question the second of the two premises. But what of the first premise? If we cannot find any reason to accept the first premise, then we do not need to accept the conclusion. How, then, would the skeptic defend his first premise?

There is a certain more general principle to which the skeptic might appeal in the attempt to defend the first premise. I will call this principle the *generalizability thesis* and formulate it as follows. "You cannot *know* that any given proposition $p$ is true unless you also know two other things. The first of these things will be a certain more *general* proposition $q$; $q$ will not imply $p$ but it will specify the conditions under which propositions of a certain type are true. And the second thing will be a proposition *r*, which enables you to *apply* this general proposition to *p*. In other words, *r* will be a proposition to the effect that the first proposition *p* satisfies the conditions specified in the second proposition *q*."

But if the generalizability thesis is true, no one knows anything. Consider the application of the thesis to a single proposition *p*. According to the thesis, if we know *p*, then we know two further propositions—a general proposition *q* and a proposition *r* that applies *q* to *p*. Applying the generalizability thesis to each of the two propositions, *q* and *r*, we obtain four more propositions; applying it to each of them, we obtain eight more propositions; . . . and so on *ad indefinitum*. The generalizability thesis implies, therefore, that we cannot know any proposition to be true unless we know all the members of such an infinite hierarchy of propositions. And therefore it implies that we cannot know any proposition to be true.

The skeptic may reply: "But in *objecting* to my general principle, you are presupposing that we *do* know something. And this begs the question." The proper rejoinder is: "But in *affirming* your general principle, you are presupposing that we *don't* know anything. And *that* begs the question."

The general reply to a skepticism that addresses itself to an entire area of knowledge can only be this: we do have the knowledge in question, and therefore, any philosophical theory implying that we do not is false. This way of looking at the matter may seem especially plausible in the present instance. It is tempting to say of skepticism, with respect to the truths of reason, what Leonard Nelson said of skepticism, with respect to the truths of mathematics. The advocate of such a skepticism, Nelson said, has invited us to "sacrifice the clearest and most lucid knowledge that we possess—indeed, the *only* knowledge that is clear and lucid *per se*. I prefer to strike the opposite course. If a philosophy, no matter how attractive or plausible or ingenious it may be, brings me into conflict with mathematics, I conclude that not mathematics but my philosophy is on the wrong track."[29] There is certainly no *better* ground for skepticism with respect to our knowledge of the truths of reason than there is for skepticism with respect to our knowledge of physical things.[30]

29 Leonard Nelson, *Socratic Method and Critical Philosophy* (New Haven: Yale University Press, 1949), p. 184.

30 "The preference of (say) seeing over understanding as a method of observation seems to me capricious. For just as an opaque body may be seen, so a concept may be understood or grasped." Alonzo Church, "Abstract Entities in Semantic Analysis," *Proceedings of the American Academy of Arts and Sciences*, 80 (1951), 100–112; the quotation is on p. 104.

And so what of the skeptic's question, "How do you know that the proposition that 2 and 4 are 6 is one that is axiomatic?" Let us recall what we said in connection with his earlier question about self-presenting states.[31] The question was: "How do you know that seeming to have a headache is a self-presenting state?" In dealing with that question, we avoided falling into the skeptic's trap. We said that the only possible answer to such a question is that we *do* know that seeming to have a headache is a self-presenting state. We should follow a similar course in the present case.

The skeptic may not be satisfied with this move and the result will be an impasse that is typical of philosophy and, in particular, of the theory of knowledge. The nature of this impasse ("the problem of the criterion") will be discussed in detail in the final chapter.

**7. "PSYCHOLOGISM"** When the skeptic and the dogmatist thus fail to reach an agreement with respect to a given area of knowledge, it is well to ask whether there may not be a misunderstanding with respect to the propositions constituting the area of knowledge. I have said that the propositions in question are concerned with certain abstract entities or eternal objects, such as properties, numbers, and propositions or states of affairs. Is it possible to interpret them in another way?

Many attempts have been made to provide such a subject-matter.

Of the attempts that have been made to provide such an interpretation, the only ones worthy of consideration are, first, the view that came to be known in the nineteenth century as "psychologism," and second, its contemporary counterpart, which we might call "linguisticism." Much of what can be said in criticism of the one can also be said, *mutatis mutandis,* in criticism of the other.

Theodore Lipps wrote, in 1880, that "logic is either a physics of thinking or it is nothing at all" and he tried to show that the truths of logic are, in fact, truths about the ways in which people think.[32] This is the view that was called "psychologism" and it was applied generally to the subject-matter of the truths of reason.

A psychologistic interpretation of "Necessarily, being red excludes being blue" might be: "Everyone is so constituted psychologically that

[31] See Chapter 2, section 8 ("A Skeptical Objection").

[32] "Die Aufgabe der Erkenntnistheori," *Philosophische Monatshefte,* Vol. XVI (1880); quoted by Husserl, in *Logical Investigations* (London: Routledge & Kegan Paul, 1970), Vol. I, p. 93. In his *Philosophie der Arithmetik* (Leipzig: C. E. M. Pfeffer, 1891), Husserl defended a version of "psychologism," but he criticizes that view in *Logical Investigations.*

if he thinks of a thing as being red, then he cannot also then think of it as being blue." And a psychologistic interpretation of the logical truth "For any propositions *p* and *q*, if *p* is true and *p* implies *q*, then *q* is true" might be: "Everyone is so constituted psychologically that if he believes that *p* is true, and if he believes that *p* implies *q*, then he cannot help but believe that *q* is true."

But obviously, these psychological sentences do not at all convey what is intended by the sentences they are supposed to translate. The psychological sentences are empirical generalizations about the ways in which people think, and as such, they can be supported only by extensive psychological investigation. Thus, Gottlob Frege said, in connection with the psychologistic interpretation of mathematics: "It would be strange if the most exact of all the sciences had to seek support from psychology, which is still feeling its way none too surely."[33] And being empirical generalizations, the psychological sentences are probable at best and are at the mercy of contrary instances. The existence somewhere of one unreasonable individual—one man who believed that some things are both red and blue, or one man who believed that a certain proposition *p* is true and also that *p* implies *q*, and who yet refused to believe that *q* is true—would be sufficient to insure that the psychological sentence is false. And we know, all too well, that there are such men. Their existence, however, has no bearing upon the truths expressed by "Necessarily, being red excludes being blue" and "Necessarily, for any propositions *p* and *q*, if *p* is true and if *p* implies *q*, then *q* is true."

In the face of such difficulties, the proponent of psychologism is likely to modify his view. He will say of sentences expressing the laws of logic and the other truths of reason, that they really express *rules of thought,* and that they are not descriptive sentences telling us how people actually do think. But to see the hopelessness of this approach, we have only to consider the possible ways of interpreting the sentence, "The laws of logic are rules of thought."

1. One interpretation would be: "The laws of logic are ethical truths pertaining to our duties and obligations with respect to thinking." In this case, the problem of our knowledge of the laws of logic is transferred

[33] *The Foundations of Arithmetic,* p. 38; Frege's work was first published in 1884. Cf. Philip E. B. Jourdain, *The Philosophy of Mr. B*rtr*nd R*ss*ll* (London: George Allen & Unwin, 1918), p. 88: "The psychological founding of logic appears to be not without analogy with the surprising method of advocates of evolutionary ethics, who expect to discover what *is* good by inquiring what cannibals have *thought* good. I sometimes feel inclined to apply the historical method to the multiplication table. I should make a statistical inquiry among school-children, before their pristine wisdom has been biased by teachers. I should put down their answers to what 6 times 9 amounts to, I should work out the average of their answers to six places of decimals, and should then decide that, at the present stage of human development, this average is the value of 6 times 9."

to the (more difficult) problem of our knowledge of the truths (if any) of ethics.

2. "The laws of logic are imperatives commanding us to think in certain ways—and imperatives are neither true nor false." This way of looking at the matter leaves us with the problem of distinguishing between valid and invalid imperatives. For there is a distinction between "Do not believe, with respect to any particular thing, both that it is red and that it is blue," and "Do not believe, with respect to any particular thing, that that thing is either red or not red." The former imperative, surely, is correct or valid, and the latter, incorrect or invalid. If we are not to fall back into skepticism, we must also say that the former is known to be valid and the latter is known to be invalid. Moreover, it is not possible to construe all of the statements of logic as imperatives. For the logician can also tell us nonimperatively such things as: If you believe that *p*, and if you believe that *p* implies *q*, and if you conform to the imperative, *modus ponens*, then you will also believe that *q*. This statement is a necessary truth. (A manual of chess, similarly, may give us certain rules in the form of imperatives: "Move the king only one square at a time." And possibly these imperatives are neither valid nor invalid. But whether or not they are valid, the chess manual will also contain true indicative sentences—sentences which are not themselves imperatives but which tell us what will happen when, in accordance with the imperatives that the manual lays down, we move the pieces into various positions. "It is impossible, if white is in such and such a position, for black to win in less than seven moves." And these statements are also necessary truths.)

3. "The laws of logic tell us which ways of believing will lead to truth and which will lead to falsehood." According to this interpretation, our two examples might be thought of as telling us respectively: "A necessary condition of avoiding false beliefs is to refrain from believing, with respect to any particular thing, both that that thing is red and also that it is blue," and "A necessary condition of avoiding false beliefs is to refrain from believing, at one and the same time, with respect to any proposition *p* and *q*, that *p* is true, that *p* implies *q*, and that *q* is false." To see that this way of formulating psychologism leaves us with our problem, let us compare it with a similar psychologistic interpretation of some other subject-matter, say, astronomy. We may say, if we like, that what the statement "There are nine planets" really tells us is that if we wish to avoid error with respect to the number of planets, it is essential to refrain from believing that there are not nine planets; it also tells us that if we wish to arrive at the truth about the number of planets, it is essential to believe that there *are* nine planets. It is not likely that in so spinning out what is conveyed by "There are nine

planets," we can throw any light upon what the astronomer thinks he knows. In any case, our problem reappears when we compare our new versions of the statements of logic with those of the statements of astronomy. The former, but not the latter, can be prefixed by, "It is necessary that," and unless we give in to skepticism (which it was the point of psychologism to avoid), we must say that the result of such a prefixing is also a statement we can know to be true.[34]

**8. "LINGUISTICISM"** A popular conception of the truths of reason at the present time is the linguistic analogue of psychologism. Versions of "linguisticism" may be obtained merely by altering our exposition of psychologism. We may replace the references to ways in which people *think* by references to ways in which they *use language,* replace the references to what people *believe* by references to what they *write* or *say,* replace "avoiding false belief" by "avoiding absurdity," and replace "rules of thought" by "rules of language." The result could then be criticized substantially, *mutatis mutandis,* as before.

Some of the versions of linguisticism, however, are less straightforward. It is often said, for example, that the sentences formulating the truths of logic are "true in virtue of the rules of language" and hence, that they are "true in virtue of the way in which we use words."[35] What could this possibly mean?

The two English sentences, "Being red excludes being blue" and "Being rational and animal includes being animal," could plausibly be said to "owe their truth," in part, to the way in which we use words. If we used "being blue" to refer to the property of being heavy, and not to that of being blue, then the first sentence (provided the other words in it had their present use) would be false instead of true. And if we used the word "and" to express the relation of disjunction instead of conjunction, then the second sentence (again, provided that the other words in it had their present use) would also be false instead of true. But as W. V. Quine has reminded us, "even so factual a sentence as 'Brutus killed Caesar' owes its truth not only to the killing but equally to our using the component words as we do."[36] Had "killed," for example, been given the use that "was survived by" happens to have, then, other things

[34] Cf. the criticism of psychologism in Husserl's *Logical Investigations,* Vol. I, pp. 90ff.; and Rudolf Carnap, *The Logical Foundations of Probability* (Chicago: University of Chicago Press, 1950), pp. 37–42.

[35] See Anthony Quinton, "The *A Priori* and the Analytic," in *Necessary Truth,* ed., Robert Sleigh (Englewood Cliffs, N.J.: Prentice-Hall, Inc., 1972), pp. 89–109.

[36] W. V. Quine, "Carnap and Logical Truth," *The Philosophy of Rudolf Carnap,* ed. P. A. Schilpp (La Salle, Ill.: Open Court Publishing Co., 1963), p. 386.

being the same, "Brutus killed Caesar" would be false instead of true.

It might be suggested, therefore, that the truths of logic and other truths of reason stand in this peculiar relationship to language: they are true "solely in virtue of the rules of our language," or "solely in virtue of the ways in which we use words." But if we take the phrase "solely in virtue of" in the way in which it would naturally be taken, then the suggestion is obviously false.

To say of a sentence that it is true *solely* in virtue of the ways in which we use words, or that it is true *solely* in virtue of the rules of our language, would be to say that the only condition that needs to obtain in order for the sentence to be true is that we use words in certain ways or that there be certain rules pertaining to the way in which words are to be used. But let us consider what conditions must obtain if the English sentence "Being red excludes being blue" is to be true. One such condition is indicated by the following sentence which we may call *T:*

> The English sentence "Being blue excludes being red" is true if, and only if, being blue excludes being red.

Clearly, the final part of *T*, the part following the second "if," formulates a necessary condition for the truth of the English sentence "Being red excludes being blue"; but it refers to a relationship among properties and not to rules of language or ways in which we use words (to suppose otherwise would be to make the mistake, once again, of confusing use and mention in language). Hence, we cannot say that the only conditions that need to obtain in order for "Being red excludes being blue" to be true is that we use words in certain ways or that there be certain rules pertaining to the ways in which words are to be used; and therefore, the sentence cannot be said to be true solely in virtue of the ways in which we use words.

## 9. ANALYZING THE PREDICATE OUT OF THE SUBJECT

The terms "analytic" and "synthetic" were introduced by Kant in order to contrast two types of categorical judgment. It will not be inaccurate to interpret "judgment," in Kant's sense, to mean the same as what we mean by "proposition." The terms "analytic" and "synthetic" are used in much of contemporary philosophy to refer instead to the types of *sentence* that express the types of judgment to which Kant referred. And perhaps Kant's view is best expressed by reference to sentences: an analytic *judgment* or *proposition* is one that is expressible in a certain type of *sentence*. But what type of sentence?

An analytic judgment, according to Kant, is a judgment in which "the predicate adds nothing to the concept of the subject." If I judge that all squares are rectangles, then, in Kant's terminology, the concept of the subject of my judgment is the property of being square, and the concept of the predicate is the property of being rectangular. Kant uses the term "analytic," since, he says, the concept of the predicate helps to "break up the concept of the subject into those constituent concepts that have all along been thought in it."[37] Since being square is the conjunctive property of being equilateral and rectangular, the predicate of the judgment expressed by "All squares are rectangular" may be said to "analyze out" what is contained in the subject. An analytic judgment, then, may be expressed in the form of an explicit redundancy: e.g., "Everything is such that if it is both equilateral and rectangular then it is rectangular." To deny such an explicit redundancy would be to affirm a *contradictio in adjecto,* for it would be to judge that there are things which both have and do not have a certain property—in the present instance, that there is something that both is and is not rectangular. Hence, Kant said that "the common principle of all analytic judgments is the law of contradiction."[38]

What might it mean to say, with respect to a sentence of the form "Everything that is an *S* is a *P*" that the predicate-term can be analyzed out of the subject-term?

One thing that might be meant is this: that what the sentence expresses can *also* be expressed in a sentence in which the predicate-term is the same as the subject term. Thus the predicate of "Everything that is a man is a rational animal" could be said to be analyzed out of the subject, since what the sentence expresses can also be expressed by saying "Everything that is a rational animal is a rational animal." But not all of the traditional examples of propositions that are analytic may be expressed in sentences wherein the subject term and the predicate-term are the same.

Consider the sentence:

1. All squares are rectangles.

What this sentence expresses may also be put as:

2. Everything that is an equilateral thing and a rectangle is a rectangle.

Sentence (2) provides us with a paradigm case of a sentence in which the predicate-term ("a rectangle") may be said to be analyzed out of the subject-term ("an equilateral thing and a rectangle").

We may note that, in sentence (2), the predicate-term is *also* part of the subject-term. Shall we say, then, that the predicate of a sentence is

[37] *Critique of Pure Reason,* A7 (Kemp Smith edition), p. 48.

[38] *Prolegomena to Any Future Metaphysics,* sec. 2.

*analyzed out* of the subject if the predicate is the same as the subject or if the subject is a conjunction of two terms one of which is the predicate? This definition would be somewhat broad, for it would require us to say that in the following sentence the predicate is analyzed out of the subject:

3. Everything that is a square and a rectangle is a rectangle.

But (3) does not exhibit the type of analysis that is to be found in (2). Thus in (3) the subject-term ("a square and a rectangle") is redundant (given "a square" in the subject we don't *need* to add "a rectangle"), but in (2) the subject-term ("an equilateral thing and a rectangle") is not redundant.

We could say, somewhat more exactly, that a predicate-term is *analyzed out* of a subject-term provided the subject-term is such that either it is itself the predicate-term or it is a conjunction of independent terms one of which is the predicate-term. But what is it for two terms to be "independent"?

We may say, of certain pairs of terms in a given language, that one of the terms *logically implies* the other in that language. Thus in English "square" logically implies "rectangle," and "red thing" logically implies "colored thing." These terms may be said to be such that in English they are *true of,* or *apply to,* certain things. And the English language is necessarily such that "rectangle" applies to everything that "square" applies to, and it is also necessarily such that "colored thing" applies to everything that "red" applies to.[39] To say, then, "*T logically implies R* in language *L*" is to say this: *L* is necessarily such that *R* applies in *L* to all those things to which *T* applies in *L*.

Now we may say what it is for two terms to be *independent*—what it is for two terms to be logically independent of each other in a given language.

Two terms are *logically independent* of each other in a given language provided only that the terms and their negations are such that no one of them logically implies the other in that language.[40] Thus "red thing"

[39] And so we do not define "English language" in terms of the people who speak it or the lands wherein it is spoken. In our use of the word "English," we may say "English is necessarily such that in it 'red' applies to things that are red." But if we defined "English" as the language spoken, say, by Englishmen or in England, we could not say "English is *necessarily* such that in it 'red' applies to things that are red." Englishmen *could* have used "blue," or any other word, in the way in which, in fact, they use "red."

[40] A term *T* may be said to be *a negation* of a term *S* in a given language *L* provided this condition holds: either *T* is part of *S*, or *S* is part of *T;* and *L* is necessarily such that, for every *x*, *T* is true of *x* in *L*, if and only if *S* is not true of *x* in *L*. Thus "nonsquare" is a negation of "square" in English (and "square" a negation of

and "square" are logically independent in English, for the four terms, "red thing," "square," "nonred thing," and "nonsquare" are such that no one of them implies the other in English.

We can now say, somewhat more exactly, what it is for the predicate-term *P,* of a sentence in a given language *L,* to be *analyzed out* of the subject-term *S.* First of all, the sentence will be an "All *S* is *P*" sentence; that is to say, the sentence will be necessarily such that it is true in *L,* if and only if, for every *x,* if *S* applies to *x* in *L,* then *P* applies to *x* in *L.* And second, either the subject-term *S* is itself the same as *P* or it is a conjunction of logically independent terms one of which is *P.*

Finally, we may define the Kantian sense of "analytic proposition" as follows: A proposition is analytic provided only it may be expressed in a sentence in which the predicate-term is analyzed out of the subject-term.

To see how the definitions may be applied, consider the following sentences, each of which may be said to express an analytic proposition, in the traditional sense of the term "analytic":

All fathers are parents.
No bachelors are married.
All dogs are dogs or cats.

What these three sentences express in English may also be put as follows:

Everything that is a male and a parent is a parent.
Everything that is a male human and a thing that is unmarried is a thing that is unmarried.
Everything that is (i) a dog or a cat and (ii) a dog or a noncat is a dog or a cat.

The last three sentences are sentences in which the predicate is analyzed out of the subject. And therefore the propositions expressed by the first sentences are all analytic.[41]

## 10. THE SYNTHETIC *A PRIORI*

Kant raised the question: Is there a synthetic *a priori?* Are there synthetic propositions that we know *a priori* to be true?

If we construe "analytic proposition" in the way in which we have tried to spell out (by reference to the predicate of a sentence being "analyzed out of" the subject), and if, as many philosophers do, we take

"nonsquare") since one is part of the other and since English is necessarily such that "square" is true of any given thing if and only if "nonsquare" is not true of that thing.

[41] If we define "father" as "male parent," and "mother" as "female parent," then we would have to say of a father who changes his sex that he becomes a mother. And analogously for a mother. Perhaps, to accommodate our language to the possibility of sex-change, we should define "father," not merely as "male parent," but as "parent who was male at the time of procreation." And analogously for "mother."

"synthetic proposition" to mean the same as "proposition which is not analytic," then Kant's question may not be particularly interesting. For, it would seem, there are many propositions which we know *a priori* and which are not analytic, in this restricted sense of the term "analytic." Among them are such propositions as:

If there are more than 7 dogs, then there are more than 5 dogs.
If there are either dogs or cows but no cows, then there are dogs.
If all men are mortal and Socrates is a man, then Socrates is mortal.

But when philosophers ask whether there are synthetic propositions that we know *a priori* to be true, they are not usually thinking of such propositions as these. They are thinking rather of propositions which can be expressed naturally in English in the form "All *S* are *P*." Given what we have said about the nature of analytic propositions, we may put the question, "Is there a synthetic *a priori?*" somewhat more exactly as follows:

Are there any propositions which are such that: (i) they are known by us *a priori;* (ii) they can be expressed in English in the form "Everything which is *S* is *P*"; and yet (iii) they are *not* such that in English their predicate-terms can be analyzed out of their subject-terms?

Let us consider, then, certain possible examples of "the synthetic *a priori,*" so conceived.

1. One important candidate for the synthetic *a priori* is the knowledge that might be expressed by saying either "Being square includes being a shape" or "Necessarily, everything that is square is a thing that has a shape." The sentence "Everything that is square is a thing that has a shape" recalls our paradigmatic "Everything that is square is a rectangle." In the case of the latter sentence, we were able to "analyze the predicate out of the subject": We replaced the subject-term "square" with a conjunctive term, "equilateral thing and a rectangle," and were thus able to express our proposition in the form:

Everything that is an *S* and a *P* is a *P*

where the terms replacing "*S*" and "*P*" are such that neither is implied by the other or by the negation of the other. But can we do this with "Everything that is square has a shape"?

The problem is to fill in the blank in the following sentence:

Everything that is a ____ and a thing that has a shape is a thing that has a shape

in the appropriate way. This means we should find a term such that: (i) the resulting sentence will express what is expressed by "Everything that is square has a shape"; (ii) the term will neither imply nor be implied by "thing that has a shape"; and (iii) the negation of our term will neither imply nor be implied by "thing that has a shape." With what term, then, can we fill the blank?

We might try "either a square or a thing that does not have a shape," thus obtaining "Everything that is (i) either a square or a thing that does not have a shape and (ii) a thing that has a shape is a thing that has a shape." But the sentence thus obtained is not one in which the predicate is analyzed out of the subject. The two terms making up the subject, namely (i) "either a square or a thing that does not have a shape" and (ii) "a thing that has a shape," are such that, in our language, any negation of the second logically implies the first (i.e., "not such as to be a thing that has a shape" logically implies "either a square or a thing that does not have a shape"). We do not have a sentence, therefore, in which the predicate can be said to be analyzed out of the subject; for the two terms making up the subject are not logically independent in our language.

What if we fill in the blank by "square," thus obtaining "Everything that is a square and a thing that has a shape is a thing that has a shape"? This will not help us, for the two terms making up the subject—"square" and "a thing that has a shape"—are such that, in our language, the first logically implies the second; hence they are not logically independent of each other; and therefore the sentence is not one in which the predicate is analyzed out of the subject. And if we drop the second term from the subject, as we can without any loss, we will be back where we started.

And so we have not found a way of showing that "Everything that is square has a shape" is analytic. But the sentence expresses what we know *a priori* to be true. And therefore, it would seem, there is at last some presumption in favor of the proposition that there is a synthetic *a priori.*

There are indefinitely many other propositions presenting essentially the same difficulties as "Everything that is square has a shape." Examples are: "Everything red is colored"; "Everyone who hears something in C-sharp minor hears a sound." The sentences express what is known *a priori,* but no one has been able to show that they are analytic.[42]

It has been suggested that the sentences giving rise to the problem of the synthetic *a priori* are really "postulates about the meanings of words," and therefore, that they do not express what is synthetic *a priori.* But if the suggestion is intended literally, then it would seem to betray

[42] Cf. C. H. Langford, "A Proof that Synthetic *A Priori* Propositions Exist," *Journal of Philosophy,* XLVI (1949), 20–24.

the confusion between use and mention that we encountered earlier. A postulate about the meaning of the word "red," for example, or a sentence expressing such a postulate, would presumably mention the word "red." It might read, "The word 'red' may be taken to refer to a certain color," or perhaps, "Let the word 'red' be taken to refer to a certain color." But "Everything that is red is colored," although it uses the words "red" and "colored," doesn't mention them at all. Thus, there would seem to be no clear sense in which it could be said really to be a "meaning postulate" or to refer in any way to words and how they are used.

2. What Leibniz called the "disparates" furnish us with a second candidate for the synthetic *a priori*. These are closely related to the type of sentence just considered, but involve problems that are essentially different. An example of a sentence concerned with disparates would be our earlier "Being red excludes being blue" or (alternatively put) "Nothing that is red is blue."[43] Philosophers have devoted considerable ingenuity to trying to show that "Nothing that is red is blue" can be expressed as a sentence that is analytic, but so far as I have been able to determine, all of these attempts have been unsuccessful. Again, it is recommended that the reader try to re-express "Nothing that is red is blue" in such a way that the predicate may be "analyzed out" of the subject in the sense we have described above.

3. It has also been held, not without plausibility, that certain ethical sentences express what is synthetic *a priori*. Thus, Leibniz, writing on what he called the "supersensible element" in knowledge, said: ". . . but to return to *necessary truths,* it is generally true that we know them only by this natural light, and not at all by the experience of the senses. For the senses can very well make known, in some sort, what is, but they cannot make known what *ought to be* or what could not be otherwise."[44] Or consider the sentence, "All pleasures, as such, are intrinsically good, or good in themselves, whenever and wherever they may occur." If this sentence expresses something that is known to be true, then what it expresses must be synthetic *a priori*. To avoid this conclusion, some philosophers deny that sentences about what is intrinsically good, or good in itself, *can* be known to be true.[45] This view will be considered briefly in the final chapter.

[43] Cf. John Locke, *Essay Concerning Human Understanding,* Book IV, Chapter 1, sec. 7; Franz Brentano, *Versuch über die Erkenntnis* (Leipzig: Felix Meiner, 1925), pp. 9–10.

[44] Quoted from *The Philosophical Works of Leibniz,* p. 162.

[45] Cf. the discussion of this question in Chapters 5 and 6 in William Frankena, *Ethics,* 2nd edition, Foundations of Philosophy Series (Englewood Cliffs, N.J.: Prentice-Hall, Inc., 1973).

**11. AN UNTENABLE DUALISM?**

But many philosophers now believe that the distinction between the analytic and the synthetic has been shown to be untenable; we should consider what reasons there might be for such a belief. Ordinarily, it is defended by reference to the following facts. (1) In drawing a distinction between analytic and synthetic sentences, one must speak of *necessity,* as we have done, or employ concepts, e.g., that of *synonymy,* that can be explicated only by reference to necessity. Thus we have spoken of a language being *necessarily* such that, if a given term applies to a thing in that language, then a certain other term also applies to that thing in that language. (2) There is no reliable way of telling, merely by observing a man's behavior, whether the language he then happens to be using is one which is *necessarily* such that if a given term applies to something in that language then a certain other term applies to that thing in that language. And (3) it is not possible, by reference merely to linguistic behavior, to say what it is for a language to be *necessarily* such that, for two given terms, if the one applies to something in that language then the other also applies to that thing in that language.[46]

But these three propositions, even if they are true, are not sufficient to yield the conclusion (4) that the distinction between the analytic and the synthetic is untenable. If we attempt to formulate the additional premise that would be needed to make the argument valid, we will see that it must involve a philosophical generalization—a generalization concerning what conditions must obtain if the distinction between the analytic and the synthetic is to be tenable. And how would the generalization be defended? This question should be considered in the light of what we have said about skepticism and the problem of the criterion. Of the philosophical generalizations that would make the above argument valid, none of them, so far as I know, has ever been defended. It is not accurate, therefore, to say that the distinction between the analytic and the synthetic has been *shown* to be untenable.

46 Cf. W. V. Quine, "Two Dogmas of Empiricism," in *From a Logical Point of View,* esp. pp. 20–37, and Morton White, "The Analytic and the Synthetic: An Untenable Dualism," in *Semantics and the Philosophy of Language,* ed. Leonard Linsky, (Urbana: University of Illinois Press, 1952), pp. 272–286.

CHAPTER FOUR

# The Indirectly Evident

---

### 1. THE JUSTIFICATION OF THE INDIRECTLY EVIDENT

Those "truths of fact" that are known but are not directly evident may be said to be indirectly evident. Hence, whatever we know about "external objects," about other people, and about the past, may be said to be indirectly evident. In considering now our justification for what is thus only indirectly evident, we should remind ourselves of what was said, at the beginning of Chapter 2, about the nature of the theory of evidence.

We said that the philosopher, in investigating the theory of evidence, makes three presuppositions. The first is that there is something that we know, and the philosopher takes it as a working hypothesis that what we know is pretty much that which, on reflection, we think we know. The second presupposition is that the things we know are so justified for us that *we* can know, on any occasion, what it is that constitutes our ground, reason, or evidence for what it is that we know. And the third presupposition is that, if we do thus have grounds or reasons for the things we think we know, then there are general principles of evidence which can be said to be satisfied by the things we think we know. Our hope is to formulate such principles.

What, then, of our justification for those propositions that are indirectly evident? We might say that they are justified in three different ways. (1) They may be justified by certain relations that they bear to what is *directly* evident. (2) They may be justified by certain relations that they bear to *each other.* And (3) they may be justified *by their own nature,* so to speak, and quite independently of the relations that they bear to anything else.

The term "foundationalism" is sometimes used for any view that emphasizes the first of these three ways. And the term "coherence theory" or "coherentism" is sometimes used for any view which emphasizes the second. But there is no use for these terms that is generally agreed upon and it may be well to avoid them.[1] And the truth of the matter, as we will see, would seem to be that what is indirectly evident may be justified in any one of these three ways.[2]

But aren't we overlooking the most obvious type of epistemic justification? Thus one might object: "The best justification we could have for a given proposition would be the fact that it comes from a *reliable source.* What could be more reasonable than accepting the deliverances of such a source—whether the source be an authority, or a computer, or a sense organ, or some kind of psychological faculty, or science itself?" The answer is, of course, that it is reasonable to put one's faith in a source which is such that one *knows* it to be reliable or one has good *ground* or *reason* or *evidence* for thinking it to be reliable. In investigating the theory of knowledge, we are concerned with the nature of the ground or reason or evidence that one might thus have for believing a source or

1 Among the views that have been labeled "foundationalism" are also the following: (1) the view that some propositions are directly evident; (2) any view that makes the three presuppositions set forth above; (3) any view that raises the questions set forth at the beginning of this chapter. Compare the critique of "foundationalism" in F. L. Will, *Induction and Justification* (Ithaca: Cornell University Press, 1974). Distinction of several senses of "foundationalism" may be found in Mark Pastin, "C. I. Lewis's Radical Phenomenalism," *Nous,* IX (1975), 407–420; and William P. Alston, "Two Types of Foundationalism," *Journal of Philosophy,* LXXIII (1976), pp. 165–185.

2 According to the theory of knowledge that is advocated by some contemporary philosophers, the view put forward in the present book is held to be one that overemphasizes "foundationalism." Compare for example: F. L. Will, *Induction and Justification;* Keith Lehrer, *Knowledge* (London: Oxford University Press, 1974); Nicholas Rescher, *The Coherence Theory of Truth* (London: Oxford University Press, 1970); Wilfrid Sellars, *Science, Perception and Reality* (London: Routledge & Kegan Paul, 1963); "Empiricism and the Philosophy of Mind," in *Empirical Knowledge: Readings from Contemporary Sources,* R. M. Chisholm and R. J. Swartz, eds. (Englewood Cliffs, N.J.: Prentice-Hall, Inc., 1973); and "Givenness and Explanatory Coherence," *Journal of Philosophy,* LXX (1973), 612–624.

an authority to be a reliable one. (Perhaps this latter point is best understood by reflecting upon the following hypothetical objection and how one might reply to it: "The best justification you can possibly have for accepting any given proposition is the fact that it is a member of the class of *true* propositions. And what could be more reasonable, after all, than restricting one's beliefs to propositions that are *true?*")

Let us begin, then, by considering the extent to which the indirectly evident might be justified by reference to what is directly evident. To what extent can we say that our knowledge of what is indirectly evident is "based upon" or "known through" the directly evident? Are there certain epistemic principles or rules of evidence which, in application to what is directly evident, will yield whatever is indirectly evident?

## 2. BEYOND THE PRINCIPLES OF LOGIC

The principles that we now seek may well include the formal principles of deductive and inductive logic. But the application of such principles to the directly evident will not of itself be sufficient to yield any of the things that we are now assuming to be indirectly evident.

The directly evident premises that are available to us at any given moment could be expressed in statements of the following sort:

I take something to be a cat on the roof.
I seem to recall that it was here before.
I am thinking about a horse.
I am trying to get across the street.
I am appeared greenly to.

The only significant deductive consequences that can be drawn from such directly evident premises will be other statements about oneself, or about thoughts, undertakings, and appearances. But the indirectly evident conclusions that we wish to derive can be expressed in statements such as:

There is a cat on the roof.
It was also here yesterday.
Part of it is green.

Hence, any principles that enable us to derive the indirectly evident from the directly evident will not be the principles of deduction.

Nor will they be the principles of induction.

Let us consider the nature of induction and ask ourselves what types of inductive argument *would* support the conclusion, "There is a cat on the roof." Broadly speaking, we may say there are two.

There are *enumerative* inductive arguments and there are also *inverse* inductive arguments. Let us first consider three enumerative inductive arguments. In each case, the premises of the argument are "factual," synthetic statements enumerating certain facts about cats and roofs or about certain things bearing a significant resemblance to cats and roofs.

There is a cat on the roof of the first house.
There is a cat on the roof of the second house.
There is a cat on the roof of the third house.
There is a fourth house.
I have no additional relevant information.
∴ It is evident for me that, there is a cat on the roof of this house.

Again:

There was a cat on the roof yesterday.
There was a cat on the roof the day before yesterday.
There was a cat on the roof the day before that.
I have no additional relevant information.
∴ It is evident for me that, there is a cat on the roof today.

Or, again

There is a sheep in front of that house, a horse in the back, a dog inside, and a cat on the roof.
There is a sheep in front of this house, a horse in the back, and a dog inside.
I have no additional relevant information.
∴ It is evident for me that there is a cat on the roof of this house.

Clearly, we have no directly evident premises to enable us to construct any such enumerative inductive argument for supporting the conclusion that a cat is on the roof. For as we have seen, every directly evident statement pertains to the thoughts or undertakings of the self or to the ways in which one is appeared to.

Induction may be construed somewhat more broadly, however. Any argument of the following sort could also be said to be an inverse inductive argument for a given hypothesis: The premises tell us, first, some of the things that would be true *if* the hypothesis were true, and secondly, that some of these things *are* true (possibly they will record the outcome of a favorable test or experiment). Thus, we might appeal to a generalization telling us some of the things that would happen if a cat were on the roof. We then perform a test or experiment to see whether these things are happening; if we find that they are, we argue that our hypothesis has been confirmed.

If there is a cat on the roof and if I stand in the garden and look toward the roof, then I will sense a cat-like appearance.
I am standing in the garden and looking toward the roof.
I sense a cat-like appearance.
I have no additional relevant information.
∴ It is evident for me that a cat is on the roof.

Other instances of this type of inductive argument may be considerably more complex, but in every case the premises will include one or more contingent statements, telling us some of the things that would follow if the conclusion, along with certain other propositions, happened to be true.

Do such premises really confer evidence for me upon the proposition that there is a cat on the roof?

Either the premises themselves have a positive epistemic status for me, or they do not. In other words, either the premises are evident or beyond reasonable doubt or acceptable or such as to have some presumption in their favor for me, or the premises are such that they have no presumption in their favor for me. Let us consider each of these possibilities.

If the premises do have some positive epistemic status for me, then our original problem is transferred to the premises. By reference to what kind of principles, then, would we exhibit the justification of the premises?

The first premise of the above argument is a contingent generalization. And it is commonly thought, at least by philosophers and scientists in the empirical tradition, that such generalizations derive whatever epistemic warrant they may have from premises, some of which at least, are perceptual propositions. But if a perceptual proposition such as "I see that there is a cat on the roof" can itself be justified only by reference to certain contingent generalizations, such as the first premise of the argument above, then we have no answer to our question about the justification of the generalization.

In short, if we say that the premises of such an argument do have some positive epistemic status for me, then the problem of the indirectly evident is transferred to the premises and we have made no progress toward its solution.

Suppose we say, then, that the premises (with the exception of the directly evident "I sense a cat-like appearance") have *no* positive epistemic status for me and thus have no presumption in their favor. How, then, can they confer positive epistemic status upon the conclusion that there is a cat on the roof? If there is *nothing* to be said in favor of the premises of our argument, then there is no ground for choosing between that argument and the one that follows:

If there is no cat on the roof and I look at a picture of a cat, then I will sense a cat-like appearance.
I am looking at a picture of a cat.
I sense a cat-like appearance.
I have no other relevant information.
∴ It is evident to me that there is no cat on the roof.

What reason could one have for preferring the first argument to the second? The only reason could be one that appeals to some kind of information that goes beyond what is directly justified. And we are left with the question: What justification do we have for thinking we have *that* information?

Similar considerations apply to any attempt to justify perceptual propositions ("There is a cat on the roof" or "I see that there is a cat on the roof") as being a part of the *best explanation* for what is indirectly evident (e.g., "I think that I see a cat on the roof"). "The acceptability of an explanation must be assessed on the basis of the degree to which the explanans as a whole is supported by factual evidence."[3] But what *is* the factual evidence that supports the explanans? This question leaves us with our original problem.

It would seem reasonable to conclude, therefore, that if the indirectly evident can be said to be made evident by what is directly evident, then there are principles of evidence other than the formal principles of deductive and inductive logic.[4]

What, then, could those principles be?

## 3. THE THEORY OF CARNEADES

If there is a solution to our problem, it is likely to be a version of the theory of Carneades of Cyrene (c. 213–129 B.C.), one of the leaders of the Platonic Academy and the most important of the "Academic Skeptics." Carneades' theory, as it is set forth by Sextus Empiricus in his *Outlines of Pyrrhonism* and in his treatise *Against the Logicians,* involves three theses concerning the "evidence of the senses."[5]

3 The quotation is from page 161 of Jaegwon Kim, "Explanation in Science," in *The Encyclopedia of Philosophy,* Vol. III (New York: The Macmillan Company & The Free Press, 1967), ed. Paul Edwards; 159–163. Compare W. C. Salmon, "Bayes' Theorem and the History of Science," *Minnesota Studies in the Philosophy of Science,* Vol. 5 (1970).

4 But one could, of course, use "inductive logic" sufficiently broadly so that any such epistemic principle might be called a "principle of inductive logic." This seems to be what Henry Kyburg has done, in criticizing the first edition of this book. He argues that considerations such as those cited above do not show that "new and different principles, other than induction and deduction, are required to pass from autobiography to natural history." But he also appeals to certain nonformal, epistemic principles. An example of such a principle is the following, which is very similar to epistemic principle B which will be formulated below: Although a given perceptual proposition might be in error, "we must have *reason* in order to doubt it seriously, i.e., in order not to accept it." See Henry Kyburg, "On a Certain Form of Philosophical Argument," *American Philosophical Quarterly,* VII (1970), 299–237; the quotations are from page 234.

5 *Sextus Empiricus,* Vol. I, Loeb Classical Library (London: William Heinemann Ltd., 1933), pp. 139–143, and Vol. II pp. 87–103. Compare Charlotte L. Stough, *Greek Skepticism: A Study in Epistemology* (Berkeley: University of California Press, 1969), esp. pp. 50–64.

1. We may put Carneades' first thesis by saying: If a man has a perception of something having a certain property *F*, then, for him, the proposition that there *is* something having that property *F* is acceptable. If he has a perception of something being a cat, for example, then, for him, the proposition that there is a cat is acceptable.[6] We could put Carneades' first principle in this general schema:

> Having a perception of something being an *F* tends to make acceptable the proposition that something is an *F*.

(We will allow Carneades such expressions as "tends to make acceptable" and "confirms." We will consider them in more detail subsequently.) But, one may ask, why use the strange expression "having a perception of something being an *F*"? Instead of "He has a perception of something being a cat," why not simply say, "He perceives something to be a cat"? And why not use "evident" instead of merely "acceptable"? If a man *perceives* something to be a cat, then, after all, he *knows* that there is a cat; the proposition is evident and not merely acceptable.

Carneades might well reply: To be sure, if a man perceives something to be *F*, then the proposition that there is an *F* is evident to him. But if our principle is expressed in this way, it can no longer be applied. For the man has no way of deciding, on any particular occasion, that he *does* perceive anything to be *F*. His experience, on any particular occasion, provides him with no guarantee that he *is* perceiving a cat.

Consider a case in which, as we sometimes put it, a man's senses have "deceived him." He takes something to be a cat and he can say honestly and sincerely that he "sees a cat"; yet what he sees is not a cat at all. His experience, at the time at which he has it, is one that he cannot distinguish from that experience which *is* correctly called "perceiving a cat"—from that experience which, if it were to occur, would make evident the proposition that the thing in question is a cat. If we use "perceive" in its ordinary way, we cannot say that, at the time of the deceptive experience, the man "perceived a cat." We must describe the experience in some other way—hence, the awkward "He has a perception of something being a cat."

If there were a way of distinguishing "veridical" perceptions, when we have them, from those that are "unveridical," we could formulate our principle by reference solely to the former. But the senses, "one and all," can "play us false"; hence, the most we can say on any particular occasion is that we are "having a perception"—a perception which may

[6] Carneades' own term is generally translated as "probable," not as "acceptable." But in view of the contemporary use of "probable" and the use that we have assigned to "acceptable," the latter is to be preferred in the present context.

or may not be veridical.[7] We can say for Carneades (he did not say it himself) that it may be directly evident to a man, on a particular occasion, that he is "having a perception of a cat," but it is never directly evident to a man that he is "perceiving a cat." Hence, if our epistemic principles are to be applied to what is "directly evident," we must refer to "having a perception of something being *F*."

2. Having delineated a class of propositions that are acceptable, Carneades now proceeds to single out a certain subclass of these propositions. Some of our perceptions, he tells us, concur and reinforce each other, "hanging together like links in a chain."[8] These perceptions he describes as being "uncontradicted and concurring"; each of them attests to the same fact and none of them casts doubt upon any of the others. In illustrating Carneades' view, Sextus cites a group of perceptions all concurring in the fact that a certain man is Socrates. "We believe that this man is Socrates from the fact that he possesses all his customary qualities—colour, size, shape, converse, coat, and his position in a place where there is no one like him." Concurrence is also illustrated in medical diagnoses: "Some doctors do not deduce that it is a true case of fever from one symptom only—such as too quick a pulse or a very high temperature—but from a concurrence, such as that of a high temperature with a rapid pulse and ulcerous joints and flushing and thirst and analogous symptoms."[9] Carneades' second thesis, then, is this: Confirmed propositions that stand in this relation of concurrence are more reasonable than those that do not. Possibly we might put this principle in our terminology as follows:

> Consider a set of propositions each one having some presumption in its favor for *S:* if each member of the set is also such that the conjunction of all the other members of the set tends to confirm it, then the members of the set are all acceptable for *S*.

As the examples suggest, Carneades must appeal to independent information—or at least to some independent set of beliefs—in order to determine whether the members of a set of perceptions happen to "concur." The perception of Socrates' coat concurs with that of his size and shape only in virtue of the fact, memory, or belief that Socrates *has* such and such a coat and such and such a size and shape. It is a defect of Carneades' account, therefore, or at least of the account that has been reported to us, that he provides no complete way of deciding *what* independent beliefs may be used in thus establishing concurrence. Perhaps

[7] Vol. II of *Sextus Empiricus,* p. 87.

[8] Ibid., para. 176, p. 95.

[9] Ibid., para. 178–179, p. 97.

we can improve upon Carneades to some extent, but any theory of evidence is likely to have a similar defect.

3. Finally, from the class of "uncontradicted and concurring" perceptions just described, Carneades singles out a further subset—those perceptions having the additional virtue of being "closely scrutinized and tested." In "testing" a perception, we "scrutinize" the condition under which it occurred. We examine the conditions of observation—the intervening medium, our sense organs, and our own state of mind. The perception survives these tests if we find the following:

> that we have our senses in good order, and that we see the object when wide awake and not asleep, and that there exists at the same time a clear atmosphere and a moderate distance and immobility on the part of the object perceived, so that because of these conditions the presentation is trustworthy, we having had sufficient time for the scrutiny of the facts observed at the seat of the presentation.[10]

In thus scrutinizing any particular perception, we appeal to other perceptions (e.g., our perception of the state of the atmosphere) and we also appeal to independent information or beliefs (e.g., the information or beliefs we must utilize in deciding whether the senses are "in good order"). Once again, Carneades fails to tell us *what* independent information and beliefs we are entitled to appeal to.[11]

Carneades' third thesis, then, is this:

> Concurrent propositions that survive such "close scrutiny and test" are more reasonable than those that do not.

Apparently, however, Carneades would not go so far as to say that they are "reasonable" in the sense of the term that we have defined, for he is not quoted as saying categorically that accepting these propositions is more reasonable than withholding them. And he denies that they are propositions that we know to be true, for, he says, they are not evident. His justification for saying they are not evident is the fact that the criteria he sets forth provide us with no guarantee of *truth:* A proposi-

[10] Ibid., para. 188, p. 103.

[11] It is interesting to note that Carneades seems to have an up-to-date view about the relation between appearances, or the ways in which we are appeared to, and what we know. He suggests, first, that "scrutiny" of appearances does not normally occur unless some belief is being tested. As Thomas Reid and others were later to say, the mind normally "passes through" the appearances and focuses directly upon the things that appear. Carneades insists, secondly, that nothing is evident to us, and therefore, he is committed to the view that our apprehension of the ways in which we are appeared to is not directly evident. Indeed, St. Augustine's remarks about appearances and skepticism, quoted on p. 27, were written in criticism of Carneades' views. But it may be that Carneades accepted what I have called "the prime mover unmoved" view of our apprehension of the ways in which we are appeared to.

tion may pass these tests and yet be false.[12] Carneades has given us, therefore, a version of skepticism.

It may be, however, that by following Carneades' general procedure, we will find what we are looking for—a way in which the indirectly evident can be said to be "known through" or "based upon" the directly evident.

The remainder of this chapter may be thought of as a preliminary sketch or outline of one possible theory of empirical evidence. We shall set forth several epistemic principles, somewhat in the manner of Carneades.

## 4. CONFIRMATION

We begin by considering the nature of confirmation.

The technical expression "*e* confirms *h*" is used to express a relation which is such that, if it holds between a proposition *e* and a proposition *h*, then it holds necessarily between *e* and *h*. Since it holds necessarily, it is sometimes described as a *logical* relation. But it is also an *epistemic* relation. For it tells us, in effect, that knowledge of *e* would give one some reason for accepting *h*. Thus the relation that *e* bears to *h*, when *e* confirms *h*, is also sometimes expressed by saying "*h* has a certain positive probability in relation to *e*."[13]

But the relation is a puzzling one. For it may be that, although a given proposition *e* confirms another proposition *h*, the conjunction of *e* with certain *other* propositions will not confirm *h*. Indeed, it may be that the wider proposition will confirm the negation of *h*. And the wider propositions may be entirely consistent with the original proposition *e*. Consider, for example, the following propositions:

(h) John is a Democrat.
(e) Most of the people in this room are Democrats, and John is in this room.
(f) Most of the people on the left side of this room are not Democrats, and John is on the left side of this room.
(g) 45 of the 50 people who arrived on time are Democrats, and John arrived on time.

[12] Cicero expresses this point by saying that "the perceptions of what is true are all of such a kind that a perception of what is false might also be of that same kind"; he adds that this fact seems to constitute the most important argument in favor of skepticism. *Academica,* Book II, Chapter 4, in *Cicero, De Natura Deorum,* The Loeb Classical Library (Cambridge: Harvard University Press, 1933), p. 565.

[13] For a general discussion of the epistemic significance of this relation, compare John Maynard Keynes, *A Treatise on Probability* (London: Macmillan Co., Ltd., 1952), Chapters 1 and 2. Compare Marsha Hanen, "Confirmation, Explanation and Acceptance," in *Analysis and Metaphysics,* ed. Keith Lehrer (Dordrecht: D. Reidel, 1975), pp. 93–128.

(i) 99 of the 100 people who voted for the measure are not Democrats, and John voted for the measure.

We may say that:

*e* confirms *h*
*e*-and-*f* confirms not-*h*
*e*-and-*f*-and-*g* confirms *h*
*e*-and-*f*-and-*g*-and-*i* confirms not-*h*.

The sense of the expression "*e* confirms *h*" might be put, somewhat loosely, by saying: "If *e* were the only thing you knew, or the only relevant evidence you had, then you would also have some reason for accepting *h*."[14] Thus one could say: "If *e* above were the only evidence you had, then you would have some reason for accepting *h;* but if, in addition to *e, f* were also a part of your evidence, and if *e* and *f* were the only evidence you had, *then* you would have some reason for accepting not-*h;* . . . and so on."

The expression "*e tends to confirm h,*" therefore, might be less misleading than "*e* confirms *h,*" and we will use it in what follows. Let us say:

D4.1 *e tends to confirm h* =Df Necessarily, for every *S,* if *e* is evident for *S* and if everything that is evident for *S* is entailed by *e,* then *h* has some presumption in its favor for *S.*[15]

We have said that it is quite possible for it to be the case that, although (1) a certain proposition *e* tends to confirm a certain proposition *h,* nevertheless (2) there is a proposition *i* which is such that the conjunction, *e* and *i,* does not tend to confirm *h*. We might say in such a case that *i* would *defeat,* or *override,* the confirmation that *e* tends to provide. This concept could be defined simply as follows:

D4.2 *i defeats* the confirmation that *e* tends to provide for *h* =Df (i) *e*

[14] Compare Rudolf Carnap: "To say that the hypothesis *h* has the probability *p* (say 3/5) with respect to the evidence *e,* means that for anyone to whom this evidence but no other relevant evidence is available, it would be reasonable to believe in *h* to the degree *p,* or, more exactly, it would be unreasonable for him to bet on *h* at odds higher than *p:* (I-*p*)." Quoted from "Statistical and Inductive Probability," in *The Structure of Scientific Thought,* ed. Edward Madden (Boston: Houghton Mifflin and Company, 1960), pp. 269–279; the quotation appears on page 270.

[15] Looking back to our example, about John being a Democrat, one may wonder whether it is *possible* for any of the propositions, *e, f, g,* and *i,* to be such that *everything* evident for *S* is entailed by it. Isn't it necessarily the case that, if any such proposition is evident for *S,* then some self-presenting proposition is also evident for *S?* If we should decide that this is so, then the definiens of D4.1 above should be modified in some such way as this: "Necessarily, for every *S,* if either (a) *e* is evident for *S* and such that everything that is evident for *S* is entailed by *e* or (b) *e* is indirectly evident for *S* and such that everything that is indirectly evident for *S* is entailed by *e,* then *h* has some presumption in its favor for *S.*"

tends to confirm *h,* and (ii) the conjunction, *e* and *i,* does not tend to confirm *h.*

Now we may turn to some of the basic principles of the theory of knowledge.

## 5. PERCEPTION AND "SELF-PRESENTATION"

We may suppose, once again, that we are dealing with a rational person, *S,* who is conducting a critique of cogency of the kind we tried to describe at the beginning of Chapter 2. *S* asks himself, with respect to various things that he knows or thinks he knows, what his justification is for thinking that he knows those things. And, it will be recalled, he asks himself these questions not to discredit or cast doubt upon his knowledge, but in order to elicit certain general principles about the nature of knowledge and of evidence.

In answer to the question, "What is my justification for thinking that I know such and such?" *S* may say: "My justification for thinking that I know such and such is the fact that I do know so and so." Let us express this briefly by saying: *S* justifies his claim or belief that he knows such and such by appeal to the proposition that he knows so and so.

Unlike Carneades, we will countenance the directly evident character of *S*'s "self-presenting states." The first of our epistemic principles is in fact a schema enabling us to abbreviate indefinitely many epistemic principles:

(A) *S*'s being *F* is such that, if it occurs, then it is self-presenting to *S* that he is *F*.

We will imagine that, to replace "*F,*" we have a list of various predicates, each of such a sort as to yield a description of a self-presenting state of *S*. Thus instances of principle A would be: "*S*'s being appeared to red is such that, if it occurs, then it is self-presenting to *S* that he is appeared to red"; "*S*'s being such that he wonders whether all men are mortal is such that, if it occurs, then it is self-presenting to *S* that he wonders whether all men are mortal."

And now, like Carneades, we may turn to perception. But we will single out two subspecies of perception and say, of the one, that it presents us with what is *reasonable,* and of the other, that it presents us with what is *evident.*

Our ordinary language makes difficulties for us at this point. For most perception words—for example, "perceive," "see," and "hear"—present us with certain problems of interpretation. How are we to interpret the sentences in which such words are followed by "that"-clauses? Consider, for example, "He perceives that a cat is on the roof," "He sees it sitting there," and "He hears it make a scratching noise." When we use our perception words in this way, do our sentences commit us to what is affirmed in their subordinate propositional clauses? Does "He perceives that a cat is on the roof" imply that there *is* a cat on the roof? Does "He sees that it is sitting there" imply that it is sitting there? And does "He hears it make a scratching noise" imply that there is something which is making a scratching noise?

The fact of the matter, unfortunately, is that the sentences are ambiguous. They may be taken either way. We may take the sentences in such a way that they do have such implications. Or we may take them in such a way that they do not. In the latter case, we may say, without contradiction, "Well, *he* perceives that a cat is there, but obviously he is hallucinating once again; he is always seeing some cat or other that isn't really there."

There would be no point in trying to decide whether one or the other of these two uses is incorrect. But if we are going to talk about perception, we should decide how we will use the terms and make sure that, once we have decided to use them in one way, we don't *also* sometimes use them in the other.

Let us use our perception words, then, in the first way. "He perceives that there is a cat there" will imply, in our use, that there is a cat there. How, then, shall we describe the state of the man who is hallucinating—the man we considered above when we said, "*He* perceives that a cat is there, but obviously he is hallucinating once again"? The simplest procedure would be to say, "He *thinks* he perceives that a cat is there" or "He *believes* that he perceives that a cat is there."

An alternative to "He thinks (or believes) he perceives that a cat is there" would be, "He *takes* there to be a cat there." Such an alternative has some advantages over "He thinks (or believes) that he perceives," for the latter expression, in its ordinary use, may suggest a kind of higher order reflection *about* one's perceptions. Grammatically, however, "He thinks (or believes) that he perceives" is more convenient, for it may be used with a "that"-clause, and it may be adapted to more specific perceptions, as "He believes that he sees" and "He believes that he hears." Hence we will use "believes that he perceives" in place of "takes." But when we say, "He believes that a cat is there," we will take it to mean simply that he has a spontaneous nonreflective experience, one that he would normally express by saying, "I perceive that. . . ."

We might now consider affirming the following principle, in the spirit of Carneades: If a person *S* believes that he perceives something to be *F*, then the proposition that he does perceive something to be *F* is one that is reasonable for him. And, for the word "perceive" in our formulation of this principle, we could substitute other verbs of the same family—for example, "observe," "see," "hear," "feel."

Such a principle was proposed in the first edition of this book. That some qualification is necessary, however, was pointed out by Herbert Heidelberger. He observed that, in its unqualified form, the principle

> . . . tells us that if a man believes that he perceives a certain object to be yellow then the proposition that he does perceive that object to be yellow and the proposition that that object is yellow are reasonable for him. But let us suppose that the following facts are known by that man: there is a yellow light shining on the object, he remembers having perceived a moment ago that the object was white, and at that time there was no colored light shining on the object. Suppose that, in spite of this evidence, he believes that he perceives that the object is yellow. It would not be correct to say that for our man the proposition that the object is yellow is a reasonable one. Merely from the fact that a man believes that he perceives something to have a certain property *F,* it does not follow, accordingly, that the proposition that that something is *F* is a reasonable one for him; for, as in our example, he may have other evidence which, when combined with the evidence that he believes that he perceives something to have *F,* may make the proposition that something is *F* highly unreasonable.[16]

Consider a slightly different example. Suppose a man believes that he perceives a sheep: that is to say, he *takes* there to be a sheep in the field before him. But he *also* has every reason to believe that his senses are deceiving him. Perhaps he has been told that he will be deceived. Or perhaps he knows that others, in the particular situation in which he happens to find himself, were deluded; they, too, thought they saw a sheep, but no sheep was there to be seen. In such a case, the proposition that he does perceive a sheep might *not* be reasonable for the man.

We could say that, if a person believes he sees something to be a sheep, and if nothing else that he knows tends to confirm the proposition that he does *not* see a sheep (i.e., if nothing that he knows tends to discredit his senses), then the proposition that he does see a sheep is one that is beyond reasonable doubt for him. In this case, we could say, more generally, that for any subject *S,* if (i) *S* believes that he is perceiving something to be *F,* and if (ii) no propositions which are acceptable for him are such that they together tend to confirm that he is *not* perceiving something to be *F,* then (iii) it is beyond reasonable doubt for *S* that he perceives something to be *F.*

In order to put this principle and certain others more briefly, we will introduce the following definition:

16 Herbert Heidelberger, in "Chisholm's Epistemic Principles," *Nous,* III (1969), 73–82; the quotation is on p. 75.

D4.3 *S* believes, *without ground for doubt,* that *p* =Df (i) *S* believes that *p* and (ii) no conjunction of propositions that are acceptable for *S* tends to confirm the negation of the proposition that *p*.

Now we may put our principle of evidence as follows:

(B) For any subject *S,* if *S* believes, without ground for doubt, that he is perceiving something to be *F,* then it is beyond reasonable doubt for *S* that he perceives something to be *F*.

We may assume that, if it is beyond reasonable doubt for *S* that he perceives something to be *F,* then it is also beyond reasonable doubt for *S* that something is *F*. For the verb "perceives" in our formula, we may substitute any other verb of the same family—for example, "sees," "hears," "feels," "observes."

By formulating principle B, then, with the qualification "without ground for doubt," we rule out the examples that had falsified the unqualified version of the principle. The first man believed he perceived something yellow; but he also had independent evidence for supposing that he was not perceiving something yellow. The second man believed he perceived a sheep in the field; but he also had independent evidence for supposing that he was not perceiving a sheep in the field. And so in neither case can we say that the man's perceptual belief was "without ground for doubt."

Are we saying, then, that before we can decide whether a perceptual proposition is reasonable, we must first find out that some *other* proposition is evident? No; we are saying, rather, that before we can decide whether a perceptual proposition is reasonable, we must first find out that certain other propositions are *not* epistemically acceptable. For principle B says that, so long as certain other propositions are not acceptable, then the man's perceptual belief is reasonable.

It should be noted that principle B gives us only a *sufficient* condition for saying that a perceptual proposition is beyond reasonable doubt. But it does not give us a *necessary* condition. From the fact that a person satisfies the conditions of the antecedent clause of principle B, it will follow that a perceptual proposition is for him beyond reasonable doubt. But nothing we have said implies that, if a perceptual proposition is thus beyond reasonable doubt for a certain subject *S,* then *S* satisfies the conditions of the antecedent clause of principle B.

Similar observations apply to other principles we will set forth.

Principle B is intended to tell us, then, that "believing that one perceives" is a source of reasonable belief. Like Carneades, we are affirming a certain faith in the senses. But we may hope that the perceptions which are thus endorsed form a slightly more respectable group than those with which Carneades began. We have assigned a higher evidential status to our perceptions than Carneades assigned to his. We say that, at the very outset, they are reasonable and not merely acceptable; these propositions of perception are such that believing them is more reasonable than withholding them.

The perceptions to which our principle refers are like the perceptions of Carneades in that they may be general and they may be negative (for example, "All the swans in the garden are white" and "There are no other animals there").

They are also like the perceptions of Carneades in that they may be false. Or more exactly, from the fact that *S* believes that he perceives a certain thing to be *F,* it will not follow that there *is* anything that is *F*. Nor will it follow that *S does* perceive something to be *F*. For as we have already noted, if a man does perceive something to be *F,* then (if we take "perceive" in the way in which we have decided to take it) he knows that there is something that is *F* and therefore, there is something that is *F*.

## 6. PERCEPTION AND THE EVIDENT

Our third epistemic principle, another thesis concerning perception, will be more bold than anything contained in Carneades' theory of evidence.

Let us return to the "proper objects" of the various senses and to the "common sensibles." The "proper objects," it will be recalled, may be illustrated by reference to the following sensible characteristics: such *visual* characteristics as blue, green, yellow, red, white, black; such *auditory* characteristics as sounding or making a noise; such *somesthetic* characteristics as rough, smooth, hard, soft, heavy, light, hot, cold; such *gustatory* characteristics as sweet, sour, salt, bitter; and such *olfactory* characteristics as fragrant, spicy, putrid, burned. The "common sensibles" are illustrated by such characteristics as movement, rest, number, figure, and magnitude, which, as Aristotle said, "are not peculiar to any sense, but are common to all."

For each of the senses there are certain *sensible relations* that are peculiar to the proper objects of that sense. The field of vision provides us with these examples: the relation that holds between any two things, *x* and *y,* when *x* is similar in color to *y;* the relation that holds among three things, *x, y,* and *z,* when *x* resembles *y* in color more than it resembles *z* in color; the relation that holds between any two things, *x* and *y,* when *x* is richer, or more saturated, in color than *y*. These relations have their analogues in the other sense spheres.

Our third principle, then, pertains to those occasions on which *S* would justify a claim to know by reference to the belief that he perceives something to have some sensible characteristic. (For brevity, we may count sensible relations as sensible characteristics.) Such occasions, we will say, provide *S* with propositions that are not only reasonable but also *evident:*

Thus we will say, in effect: If being *F* is a sensible characteristic, and if *S* believes that he perceives something to be *F,* then the proposition that he does perceive something to be *F,* as well as the proposition that something is in fact *F,* is one that is evident for *S*. Variants of this principle have been proposed by A. Meinong and H. H. Price. Where I have said that beliefs pertaining to the perception of sensible characteristics "tend to make certain propositions evident," Meinong says that such perception yields "presumptive evidence" (*Vermutungsevidenz*) and Price says it yields only "*prima facie* evidence."[17] One might say that believing one sees something to be red tends to make evident the proposition that something is red.

But instead of proceeding in this way, we will introduce a schematic principle, as we did in the case of principle A. We will say:

(C) For any subject *S,* if *S* believes, without ground for doubt, that he is perceiving something to be *F,* then it is evident for *S* that he perceives something to be *F.*

In the place of "*F,*" we substitute any predicate (for example, "red" and "blue") connoting a sensible characteristic. We may assume that, if it is evident for *S* that he perceives something to be *F,* then it is also evident for him that something is *F.* As in the case of principle *B,* other perception verbs may replace "perceives" in the formulation of this principle.

What we are now saying must be distinguished from our earlier thesis about appearances, or the ways in which a man is appeared to. We said that if *S* is appeared to red, or blue, or green, or yellow, then it is directly evident to *S* that he is appeared to in that way. But we are now speaking not merely of the ways in which *S* is appeared to, but also of things that appear to *S*. We are saying that taking something to be red, or blue, or green, or yellow, tends to make evident there *being* something that is red, or blue, or green, or yellow. This would also hold true for other sensible characteristics and relations.

[17] See A. Meinong, *Über die Erfahrungsgrundlagen unseres Wissens* (1906); republished in *Alexius Meinong Gesamtausgabe,* Band V, Rudolf Haller and Rudolf Kindinger, eds. (Graz: Akademische Druck- und Verlagsanstalt, 1973); H. H. Price, *Perception* (New York: Robert M. McBride & Co., 1933), p. 185. Compare Roderick M. Chisholm, *Perceiving: A Philosophical Study* (Ithaca: Cornell University Press, 1957), Chapter 6.

## 7. MEMORY

When Carneades sets out to establish "concurrence" and to "test and scrutinize" his perceptions, he makes use of certain independent information. Or more exactly, he appeals to certain beliefs that he has—beliefs about the properties of the things that he is perceiving, about the condition of the intervening medium, about his own psychological and physiological state. But he fails to tell us anything about the credentials of these independent beliefs. Clearly, this gap in his account should be filled by reference to *memory*.

The word "memory" presents us with a terminological difficulty analogous to that presented by "perception." Consider a case in which, as one might say, a man's memory has "deceived him": the man would have said, honestly and sincerely, that he remembered a certain event to have occurred; actually, the event did not occur at all. Such deceptions of memory are common; "we remember remembering things and later finding them to be false."[18] But if we say "what he remembered is false," the ordinary interpretation of the word "remember" will render what we say contradictory; hence, if we wish to take "remember" in this ordinary way, we must express the fact in question by saying, "What he *thought* he remembered is false." And of those cases where one's memory is not thus deceptive, we may say that "what he thought he remembered is true."

Let us introduce the expression "unveridical memory" and use it in the way we have just been using "unveridical perception." A person may be said to have an *unveridical memory* if he mistakenly thinks he remembers a certain thing. We may also say that he remembers that thing unveridically.

Since both memory and perception are capable of playing us false, we run a twofold risk when we appeal to the memory of a perception. Let us suppose that *S* defends his claim to know that "A cat was on the roof" by saying he thinks he remembers having perceived one there. The situation presents us with four possibilities. (1) The present memory and the past perception are both veridical: he did think he perceived a cat and what he saw was, in fact, a cat. (2) He correctly remembers having thought he saw a cat; but what he saw was not a cat. In this case, the fault lies with the past perception and not with the present memory. (3) He incorrectly remembers having thought he saw a cat; but what he really thought he saw, at the time, was a squirrel, and in fact it was a squirrel that he saw. In this case, the fault lies with the present memory

[18] C. I. Lewis, *An Analysis of Knowledge and Valuation* (La Salle, Ill.: Open Court Publishing Co., 1946), p. 334.

and not with the past perception. (4) He incorrectly remembers having thought he saw a cat; but what he thought he saw, at the time, was a squirrel, and the perception was unveridical, for there was no squirrel there at all. In this case, the fault lies both with the present memory and the past perception. As we know, however, memory, by a kind of happy failure if not an act of dishonesty, may correct the past perception: The man thought he saw a squirrel but it was in fact a cat, and now he thinks he remembers that he thought he saw a cat. Ordinary language provides us with no clear way of distinguishing these different types of deception, and memory is likely to receive more blame than it deserves. But it would seem to be clear, in general, that we should assign a lower degree of evidence to the deliverances of memory.

Where we said, in effect, that one type of perceptual belief made something *reasonable,* and another type of perceptual belief made something *evident,* let us now replace "reasonable" and "evident," respectively, by "acceptable" and "reasonable." We may add, then, two principles pertaining to memory.

And so we will be saying, in effect, that if *S* seems to remember perceiving something to be *F,* then the proposition that he does remember perceiving something to be *F* is one that is reasonable for *S*. Our first principle pertaining to memory will be this:

(D) For any subject *S,* if *S* believes, without ground for doubt, that he remembers perceiving something to be *F,* then the proposition that he does remember perceiving something to be *F* is one that is acceptable for *S*.

We may assume that, if the proposition that *S* would express in English by saying "I remember perceiving something to be *F*" is one that is acceptable for him, then so, too, is the proposition that he did perceive something to be *F,* as well as the proposition that something was *F*.

Perhaps there is reason to distinguish between "remembering perceiving" and "remembering having perceived." Thus one might be able to say, "I remember having perceived someone leaving the bank" even though one cannot say, "I remember perceiving someone leaving the bank"; in such a case, presumably, the details of the perception have been forgotten and one remembers only that one *did* perceive. If this distinction is a tenable one, then we should note that principle D applies to remembering perceiving and need not apply to remembering having perceived.

We will assume, in effect, that, if the property being *G* is a sensible characteristic, then seeming to remember perceiving something to be *G* tends to make reasonable the propositions that one does remember perceiving something to be *G*, that one perceived something to be *G*, and that something was *G*. Our second principle pertaining to memory will be a schema, wherein the letter "*F*" may be replaced by any predicate (e.g., "red" or "blue") which connotes a sensible characteristic.

(E) For any subject *S*, if *S* believes, without ground for doubt, that he remembers perceiving something to be *F*, then it is beyond reasonable doubt for *S* that he does remember perceiving something to be *F*.

Variants of these two principles have been suggested by other philosophers: Meinong held that our memory judgments, as he called them, possess "immediate presumptive evidence." Russell has said that every memory should "command a certain degree of credence." And Lewis said that "whatever is remembered, whether as explicit recollection or merely in the form of our sense of the past, is *prima facie* credible because so remembered."[19]

There is still more that can be said in behalf of memory.

If our memories of sensible perceptions are reasonable, so, too, must be our memories of the "self-presenting states" discussed in Chapter 2. Thus I may think that I remembered that I believed, or desired, or hoped, or loved, or that I undertook a certain thing, or that I was appeared to in a certain way. Don't such facts tend to make reasonable the propositions that I thus seem to remember? Let us add, therefore, another schematic principle. The expression "*F*" which appears in this principle may be replaced by any expression yielding a description of what we have called a self-presenting state:

(F) For any subject *S*, if *S* believes, without ground for doubt, that he remembers being *F*, then it is beyond reasonable doubt for *S* that he does remember that he was *F*.

We have said that our perception of things in motion, or at rest, and our perception of events in temporal succession are sources of what is evident. In saying this, we have conceded the evident character of "fresh memory" or "proterasthesis"—our apprehension of the "immediate past."[20] Whenever we perceive a thing to be in motion, or to be at rest, and

[19] Meinong, "Toward an Epistemological Assessment of Memory," in *Empirical Knowledge: Readings from Contemporary Sources,* Chisholm and Swartz, eds., pp. 253–270; the paper was first published in 1896. Bertrand Russell, *An Inquiry into Meaning and Truth* (New York: W. W. Norton & Co., 1940), pp. 192–202; C. I. Lewis, *An Analysis of Knowledge and Valuation,* p. 334.

[20] Franz Brentano uses the term "*Proterästhese*" in this connection; Russell uses "immediate past." See Brentano's *Die Lehre vom richtigen Urteil* (Bern: A. Francke, 1956), p. 158, and Russell's *Inquiry into Meaning and Truth,* p. 192.

whenever we perceive a succession of events, as we do when we listen to a melody or to a conversation, we perceive one event as being temporally prior to another. When we do perceive one event as being temporally prior, then we perceive the former as being past. Whether this apprehension of the immediate past is to be called "memory" may be a matter only of terminology. But if we do call it "memory," then we may say that what we thus remember, or think we remember, is something that is *evident*.[21]

And so we have replaced Carneades' first principle, which states that all of our "perceptions" are acceptable, by several different theses about perception and memory. In one respect, as we have noted, our several theses are epistemically more rigorous than was the first thesis of Carneades. For if we follow the account of Carneades that has been handed down to us, we may be required to say that, for *S,* "There is a thief in the garden" may express a perception and hence be acceptable. In another respect, our several theses are epistemically more lenient than the first thesis of Carneades. For they allow us to say of certain types of propositions not only that such propositions are acceptable, but also that they are reasonable, and that some of them—those that pertain to sensible characteristics and relations—are evident.

But our principles do not yet allow us to say, of Mr. *S,* that it is evident to him that a cat is on the roof.

We must return, then, to the concept of *confirmation*.

## 8. CONFIRMATION AND CONCURRENCE

Appealing now to the concept of confirmation, and in particular to "*e* tends to confirm *h*," which was defined in section 4 above (D4.1), we will first note how to add to the class of propositions that have some positive epistemic status for our subject *S*.

Since whatever is evident is also reasonable and since whatever is reasonable is also acceptable, we may say that all of the propositions countenanced by the principles we have set forth are acceptable. We may now apply the concept of confirmation and say that if the conjunction of all of those propositions that are acceptable tends to confirm a given proposition, then that proposition has some presumption in its favor.[22] Hence, we may add the following to our principles:

(G) If the conjunction of all those propositions *e,* such that *e* is acceptable

[21] And if we call it "memory" we should not cease to call it "perception." "Hearing one note to precede another" may not be analyzed into "hearing the one note and subsequently hearing another" or into "remembering one note and hearing another."

[22] Given what we will say in the following chapter about propositions and states of affairs, it would be more accurate to replace "proposition," in (G) and (H), by "state of affairs."

for *S* at *t* tends to confirm *h*, then *h* has some presumption in its favor for *S* at *t*.

The class of propositions that thus have some presumption in their favor for *S* may now include a vast number of inductive hypotheses and thus go considerably beyond the content of memory and perception. For example, they may include propositions about cats and roofs.

By applying Carneades' concept of *concurrence* to this expanded class of propositions, we are also able to expand the class of propositions that are to be countenanced as being *beyond reasonable doubt* for *S* at *t*. When Carneades said that a set of propositions might be concurrent, he meant that each member of the set would support, and also be supported by, the other members of the set. We could say that any set of propositions that are mutually consistent and logically independent of each other is concurrent provided that each member of the set is confirmed by the conjunction of all the members of the set.[23] More exactly:

D4.4 *A* is a set of *concurrent* propositions =Df *A* is a set of two or more propositions each of which is such that the conjunction of all the others tends to confirm it and is logically independent of it.

There will conceivably be many sets of concurrent propositions among those propositions that now have some presumption in their favor for *S*. Let us consider, then, the following principle:

(H) Any set of concurring propositions, each of which has some presumption in its favor for *S*, is such that each of its members is beyond reasonable doubt for *S*.

In other words, if among the propositions having some presumption in their favor for *S*, there is a set related by mutual support, then each of those propositions is beyond reasonable doubt for *S*. This principle is somewhat bold, epistemically, but boldness is in order if we are to continue to hold that skepticism is false.

The following is an example, slightly oversimplified, of what might be such a concurrent set: "There is a cat on the roof today; there was one there yesterday; there was one there the day before yesterday; there was one there the day before that; and there is a cat on the roof almost every day." We may assume that the first statement expresses a present perception and, therefore, that it expresses what is reasonable (hence,

[23] Cf. the definition of "coherence" in H. H. Price's *Perception*, p. 183, and the definition of "congruence" in C. I. Lewis, *An Analysis of Knowledge and Valuation*, p. 338; Lewis discusses the logical properties of this concept in detail. See also Roderick Firth, "Coherence, Certainty, and Epistemic Priority," in *Empirical Knowledge*, Chisholm and Swartz, eds., pp. 459–470; Nicholas Rescher, *The Coherence Theory of Truth* (London: Oxford University Press, 1973), pp. 53–71; and Keith Lehrer, *Knowledge* (London: Oxford University Press), pp. 154–186.

also acceptable) by principle B; we may assume that the second, third, and fourth statements express certain memories and, therefore, that they express what is acceptable by principle D; and we may assume that the final statement is confirmed by the set of all of those statements that are empirically acceptable for *S* and, therefore, that it expresses what is acceptable by principle G. Each of the five propositions thus formulated may be said to be confirmed by the set of all the others. They are mutually consistent; hence, they are concurrent; and therefore, they are all reasonable by principle H.

Carneades had spoken of concurring presentations as hanging together like "links in a chain." But Meinong's figure may be more illuminating: "One may think of playing cards. No one of them is capable of standing by itself, but several of them, leaned against each other, can serve to hold each other up."[24] Each of the propositions in our concurrent set must be acceptable on its own if we are to derive reasonability from concurrence, just as each of the members of a house of cards must have its own degree of substance and rigidity if the house is not to collapse. (We may be reluctant to compare reasonability with a house of cards. In this event, Meinong has two other figures for us: the arch of a bridge, and a stack of weapons in the field.)

And finally, from our concurrent set of propositions—now reasonable as well as acceptable—we extract still another class of propositions; the members of this new class will be countenanced as being evident.

(I) If *S* believes, without ground for doubt, that he perceives something to be *F*, and if the proposition that there is something that is *F* is a member of a set of concurrent propositions each of which is beyond reasonable doubt for *S*, then it is evident for *S* that he perceives something to be *F*.

This principle is even more audacious than principle H.

The set of concurrent propositions cited just above includes the perceptual proposition "A cat is on the roof." Hence, in virtue of principle I, and the definition of knowledge to be proposed in Chapter 6, we may be able to say, at last, that *S* *knows* that there is a cat on the roof.

## 9. CONCLUSION

Here, then, we have the beginning of a theory of evidence. It is by no means complete. Any complete theory would include the canons of inductive logic.[25] And it would

[24] A. Meinong, *Über Möglichkeit und Wahrscheinlichkeit* (1915), p. 465; this work now constitutes Volume VI of *Alexius Meinong Gesamtausgabe* (Graz: Akademisches Druck- und Verlagsanstalt, 1972), Rudolf Haller and Rudolf Kindinger, eds.

[25] A complete theory of empirical evidence would also deal with this question: Under

include many additional epistemic principles. Thus, in our formulation of the principles pertaining to perception and memory, we used the expression, "without ground for doubt"; we said in D4.3 that a person believes a proposition "without ground for doubt" provided he believes nothing that tends to confirm the negation of that proposition. Hence an adequate theory of evidence would set forth certain general principles concerning what propositions would tend to confirm that one is being deceived by one's senses or memory.[26] But any adequate theory of evidence, I believe, would contain principles very much like those that we have set forth.

We said, at the beginning of this chapter, that propositions that are not directly justified may be justified in one or another of three different ways. (1) They may be justified in virtue of the relation they bear to what is *directly evident*. (2) They may be justified by certain relations they bear to *each other*. And (3) they may be justified by *their own nature* and thus quite independently of the relations they may bear to other propositions.

Looking back to the general principles we have formulated, we may now note the way in which all three phases of justification are here exemplified. (1) Every proposition we are justified in believing is justified, in part, because of some relation that it bears to the directly evident.[27] (2) The reference to *concurrence* in our final two principles

---

what conditions, if any, would confirmation by a set of evident propositions make another proposition evident? It would be absurd to suppose that whenever we find a given hypothesis is confirmed by our evidence, we are then justified in adding that hypothesis to our evidence and using it as a basis for additional inductions. The set of premises (*e*) that Jones is one of the Christians in Goleta, that 51 of the 100 Christians in Goleta are Protestants, and that 26 of the Protestants there are Presbyterians could be said to confirm (*h*) that Jones is a Protestant. If now we add *h* to our evidence, our increased evidence base will then confirm (*i*) that Jones is a Presbyterian. But under these conditions it would be absurd to widen our evidence base still further and count "Jones is Presbyterian" as a proposition that is evident. Yet it is often presupposed in writings on the philosophy of science that there are some conditions under which confirmation by a set of evident propositions can thus confer evidence upon a proposition that the set does not entail. An unsolved "problem of induction" is that of saying just what these conditions might be.

26 I have discussed some of these principles in "On the Nature of Empirical Evidence," in *Empirical Knowledge*, Chisholm and Swartz, eds., pp. 224–249; see especially pp. 245–247. A more thoroughgoing attempt to set forth such principles may be found in John Pollock, *Knowledge and Justification* (Princeton: Princeton University Press, 1974); see especially Chapters 5 through 8.

27 This is true even of the axioms we discussed in the previous chapter. We said that a proposition is an *axiom* for a given subject *S* provided, first, it is axiomatic (it is necessarily such that if one accepts it then it is certain), and, second, *S* does accept it. But the proposition that he *does* accept the axiom will be one that is self-presenting for him. We could say, in Kant's terms, that *S*'s knowledge of the axiom "begins with" what is self-presenting even though it does not "arise out of" what is self-presenting.

recognizes the importance of the mutual support that is provided, in part, by the logical relations that certain propositions bear to each other. And finally, (3) some propositions are such that, by their very nature, they tend to provide a justification for propositions about what one thinks one is perceiving and about what one thinks that one remembers.

## CHAPTER FIVE

# Truth

**1. WHAT IS TRUTH?** Our question is easy to answer if we allow ourselves two metaphysical assumptions, but otherwise it is not. The assumptions are: first, that there are states of affairs, some of which occur or obtain and some of which do not occur or obtain; and second, that there are attributes or properties, some of which are exemplified or instantiated and some of which are not exemplified or instantiated. We may assume that what philosophers sometimes call "propositions" are a subspecies of states of affairs—those states of affairs, namely, which are necessarily such that either they always obtain or they never obtain.[1]

Following a suggestion made by Leibniz, we could say that a state of

1 Concerning propositions and states of affairs, compare the following writings: Bernard Bolzano, *Theory of Science,* ed. Rolf George (Oxford: Basil Blackwell, 1972), pp. 19–42; G. Frege, "Compound Thoughts," *Mind,* LXVII (1963), 1–17; C. A. Baylis, "Facts, Propositions, Exemplification and Truth," *Mind,* LVII (1948), 459–479; C. I. Lewis, *An Analysis of Knowledge and Valuation* (La Salle, Ill.: The Open Court Publishing Company, 1946), pp. 48–70; Roderick M. Chisholm, *Person and Object: A Metaphysical Study* (La Salle, Ill.: The Open Court Publishing Company; London: George Allen and Unwin, 1976), Chapter 4.

affairs is a thing which is such that it is possible that there is someone who accepts it.[2] (The definitions that are proposed in this chapter are put more formally in the Appendix.)

Propositions, we have said, are a subspecies of states of affairs—those which are necessarily such that either they always obtain or they never obtain.

A proposition, we may now say, is *true* if and only if it obtains. And it is *false* if and only if it does not obtain. Hence every proposition is such that either it is true or it is false, and no proposition is such that it is both true and false.

And a *fact,* we could say, is a true proposition.

There is no question, then, about the sense in which true propositions may be said to "correspond with" facts. They correspond with facts in the fullest sense that is possible, for they *are* facts.

What is a true belief?

By reference to states of affairs and to properties, we may distinguish two kinds of belief—belief *de dicto* and belief *de re.*

If I believe, *de dicto,* that the tallest man is wise, then that state of affairs which is the tallest man being wise is one that I accept. If you ask me what I believe and if I reply honestly and accurately, I will say, "I believe that the tallest man is wise." And I could believe, *de dicto,* that the tallest man is wise, even if there were no tallest man.

If I believe, *de re,* with respect to the tallest man, that he is wise, then the property of being wise is one that I attribute to the tallest man. In this case, one of the things that may be said about the tallest man is this: he is such that I believe him to be wise. Hence the tallest man cannot be believed by me to be wise unless there is a tallest man. But he may be believed by me to be wise without my knowing that he is the tallest man or even that there is a tallest man. If you ask me whether I believe that the tallest man is wise, I may say, quite honestly and sincerely, that I do not, but pointing to the tallest man, I may add, quite consistently, "I believe that he is wise."

To have a belief *de dicto,* then, is to accept a certain state of affairs. And to have a belief *de re* is to attribute a certain property to something.[3]

And now we may say what a true belief is. A man has a *true belief de dicto,* if and only if, he accepts a state of affairs which obtains. And he

[2] See Bolzano, *Theory of Science,* p. 76. Leibniz's suggestion, which Bolzano interprets in accordance with the definiens above, was concerned with *propositions* rather than with states of affairs.

[3] It may yet be, however, that belief *de re* may be thought of a species of belief *de dicto.* I have defended this view in "Knowledge and Belief: 'De Dicto' and 'De Re,'" *Philosophical Studies,* 33 (1975), 9–28.

has a *true belief de re,* if and only if, he attributes a property to something that has that property.

A belief is *false,* obviously, if and only if it is a belief that is not true: one accepts a state of affairs that does not obtain, or one attributes a property to something that doesn't have that property.

We have said that every proposition is either true or false and that no proposition is both. From these principles and what we have said about belief, it follows that every belief *de dicto* is either true or false and none is both.

We may also say that, for every thing and every property, either the thing has the property or the thing does not have the property, and the thing is not such that it both has and does not have the property. From these principles and what we have said about belief, it follows that every belief *de re* is either true or false and none is both.

## 2. ASSERTIONS AND SENTENCES AS VEHICLES OF TRUTH

Some of the things we have said about believing may now be said, *mutatis mutandis,* about assertions and sentences.

Thus one may be said to make a *de dicto* assertion if and only if one asserts a certain state of affairs or proposition. A *de dicto* assertion is *true* if and only if the state of affairs that is asserted is one that obtains, and it is *false* if and only if the state of affairs that is asserted is one that does not obtain. One may be said to make a *de re* assertion if and only if one ascribes a property to something. Such an assertion is *true* if and only if the thing has the property, and *false* if and only if the thing does not have the property.

We may readily endorse, then, Aristotle's classic statement: "To say of what is that it is not, or of what is not that it is, is false, while to say of what is that it is, or of what is not that it is not, is true."[4] But perhaps we are justified in adding that this statement gives us only a part of the story.

What of the truth of *sentences?*

The following would be a simple account of the truth of sentences: A sentence is *true* provided only (i) it expresses a certain state of affairs and (ii) that state of affairs obtains. And a sentence is *false* provided only (i) it expresses a certain state of affairs and (ii) that state of affairs does not obtain.

But we should modify this account in two ways.

We should distinguish sentence-tokens from sentence-types. (Suppose I write: "All men are mortal," "All men are mortal," and "All Greeks

[4] *Metaphysics,* 1011b.

are men." How many sentences have I written—two or three? The proper way to deal with this question is to note that "sentence" may be ambiguous as between "sentence-type" and "sentence-token," and then to observe that I have written *three* sentence-tokens and *two* sentence-types.) If you are hungry and I am not but we both utter the sentence-token "I am hungry," then the one that you utter will be true and the one that I utter will be false. We might say that a sentence-type is true provided that some of its tokens are true and that a sentence-type is false provided that some of its tokens are false. But then we would have to say that the sentence-type "I am hungry" is both true and false. We can avoid this consequence if we restrict our account to sentence-tokens.

There is a second restriction we should make in our account of the truth of sentences. For one and the same sentence-token may express one thing in one language and another thing in another language. And so it is possible that you may utter a token that is true in your language and false in mine. Hence one and the same token is true and false at one and the same time. Therefore, we should restrict our account to sentences *in* languages, saying what it is for a sentence to be true, or to be false, in a given language *L*.

And so this will be our account of the truth and falsity of sentences: A sentence-token is *true* in a given language *L* provided only (i) it expresses a certain state of affairs in *L* and (ii) that state of affairs obtains. And a sentence-token is *false* in a given language *L* provided only (i) it expresses a certain state of affairs in *L* and (ii) that state of affairs does not obtain.[5]

Our account of true and false *belief* implied that every belief—whether *de re* or *de dicto*—is either true or false. And our account of true and false *assertion* implied that every assertion—whether *de re* or *de dicto*—is either true or false. But our account of true and false *sentence-tokens* does *not* imply that every sentence-token is either true or false. It leaves open the possibility that some sentence-tokens are neither true nor false. Thus if a sentence-token does not express a state of affairs and does not predicate a property of anything, then it is neither true nor false. But to say that there are such sentence-tokens that are neither true nor false

[5] Conceivably, we might want to distinguish *de dicto* and *de re* sentence-tokens. ("All men are mortal" is a *de dicto* English sentence-token, expressing the state of affairs of all men being mortal. The sentence-token "This is to be used for emergency only," painted on a door, is a *de re* sentence-token, saying, with respect to the door, that it is to be used for emergency only.) If we make this distinction, then the above account, which holds only of *de dicto* sentence-tokens, should be supplemented by the following: A *true de re* sentence-token in *L* is a *de re* sentence-token in *L* which, in *L*, predicates a property of something that has that property. And a *false de re* sentence-token in *L* is one which, in *L*, predicates a property of something that does not have that property.

is not to deny what is axiomatic or *a priori*. For what is axiomatic or *a priori* is not the proposition that every sentence-token is either true or false. What is *a priori* are, rather, the propositions, first, that every *proposition* is either true or false, and, second, the proposition that, for every thing and every property, either the thing has the property or the thing doesn't have the property.

Failure to see these latter points has led many philosophers to suppose that there are genuine paradoxes about truth. A test for any theory of truth will be the degree of success it has in dealing with what have thus been thought to be genuine paradoxes.

**3. THE EPIMENIDES** One of the oldest of the supposed paradoxes is "the Epimenides," or "the Liar," so-called because Epimenides of Crete is reported to have said that all Cretans were liars.[6] If a man says, "I am now lying," is he saying something that is true or something that is false? Either possibility seems to lead to a contradiction.

We bring the problem into sharper focus if we consider a man who says, more baldly, "What I am saying is false." And so let us formulate it this way: "Suppose (i) a man says, 'What I am saying is false.' Then (ii) if what he is saying is true, then things are not as he says they are, so what he is saying is false. But (iii) if what he is saying is false, then things are as he says they are, and so what he is saying is true. But (iv) what he is saying is either true or false. Therefore (v) what he is saying is both true and false. How can this be?"

The expression "what he is saying" may be read either as "his assertion" or as "the sentence-token he is uttering." Let us consider each possibility.

The first would be this: "Suppose (i) a man says, 'What I am saying is false.' Then (ii) if his assertion is true, then his assertion is false. And (iii) if his assertion is false, then his assertion is true. But (iv) his assertion is either true or false. Therefore (v) his assertion is both true and false. How can this be?"

The doubtful step in the argument is (iv)—"His assertion is either true or false." But how can *this* be the doubtful step? Haven't we said that every assertion is either true or false? The answer is that, if a man utters the words, "What I am saying is false," and takes them in their ordinary English sense, then, even if his utterance is sincere and made with conviction, he is not *asserting* anything. (After all, what could he

[6] St. Paul wrote: "One of themselves, a prophet of their own, said, 'Cretans are always liars, evil beasts, lazy gluttons.' This testimony is true. . . ." *Titus,* I, 12–13.

be telling us if he said only, "What I'm saying is false"?) But if he is not asserting anything, then of course we can deny what is expressed by "His assertion is either true or false."

Let us now replace "his assertion" by "the sentence-token he is uttering." Our formulation of the problem now becomes: "Suppose (i) a man says, 'What I am saying is false.' Then (ii) if the sentence-token he is uttering is true, then the sentence-token he is uttering is false. And (iii) if the sentence-token he is uttering is false, then the sentence-token he is uttering is true. But (iv) the sentence-token he is uttering is either true or false. Therefore (v) the sentence-token he is uttering is both true and false. How can this be?"

Once again we would deny step (iv)—"The sentence-token he is uttering is either true or false." We could deny "His *assertion* is either true or false" on the ground that he is not asserting anything. But we cannot deny "The sentence-token he is uttering is either true or false" on the ground that he is not uttering any sentence-token, since he *is* uttering, "What I am saying is false." We must say, rather, that the sentence-token he is uttering is neither true nor false, and then we avoid the contradiction. And to say this, as we have noted, is not to deny anything that is axiomatic or *a priori*. For it is not axiomatic or *a priori* that every sentence-token is either true or false. Some sentence-tokens don't express any proposition or predicate any property of anything, and those sentence-tokens are neither true nor false.

The point will become clearer if we consider other versions of the problem.

## 4. PUZZLES ABOUT SENTENCE-TOKENS

We have construed the Epimenides as a paradox about assertions. Suppose now we consider it, as is usually done in writings of contemporary philosophers, as a paradox about sentence-tokens.

The simplest version of the paradox, when so construed, may be put by reference to the sentence-token that immediately follows on this page:

(a) Sentence-token (a) is false.

One may propose the following argument:

(i) If sentence-token (a) is false, then what it says is true and therefore it is true;
(ii) If sentence-token (a) is true, then what it says is false and therefore it is false;
(iii) But sentence-token (a) is either true or false.
(iv) Therefore sentence-token (a) is both true and false.

If we adopt the procedure we followed in the case of the second version of the Epimenides just discussed, we will simply deny the third premise and say, instead, that sentence-token (a) is neither true nor false.

But consider now a sentence-token that seems to say of itself, not that it is *false,* but that it *isn't true.* We would have an instance of this in the sentence-token (b) that immediately follows:

(b) Sentence-token (b) is not true.

In dealing with the previous puzzle, we could say, "Some sentence-tokens are neither true nor false" without violating any principles of logic or metaphysics. But we would violate a basic principle of logic if we were to say that some sentence-tokens are neither *true* nor *not true.* For this would be counter to the general principle, formulated above, according to which, for every thing and every property, either the thing has the property or the thing does not have the property. Let us consider, then, how the present version of the paradox might go.

(i) If sentence-token (b) is not true, then what it says is true, and therefore it is true.
(ii) If sentence-token (b) is true, then what it says is not true, and therefore it is not true.
(iii) Sentence-token (b) is either true or not true.
(iv) Sentence-token (b) is true and sentence-token (b) is not true.

It is clear that the conclusion follows from the premises and that we cannot, as before, reasonably deny the third premise.

But let us look more carefully at premises (i) and (ii). Each of them presupposes that there *is* something that sentence-token (b) says. In other words, each of them presupposes that there is a state of affairs that is expressed by sentence-token (b). But what if we said that there is *no* such state of affairs? Then we could deny both (i) and (ii) and hence avoid the contradictory conclusion.

We can be confident of the following assertions:

(c) Sentence-token (b) is not true.
(d) Sentence-token (c) is true.

But sentence-token (b) and sentence-token (c) are two tokens of the same type. "How can it be," one may ask, "that two sentence-tokens of the same type may be such that one of them is true and the other one not?" We have already seen that two sentence-tokens of the same type may be such that one of them is true and the other not. "I am hungry," when said by one man may be true and when said by another may be false; or it may be true when said by one man at one time and false when said by that same man at another time. "But in those cases," one may object, "the subject-term 'I' of the sentence-tokens is used in one case to refer to one thing and in another case to refer to another thing. Or it is used in one case to refer to one thing at one time and in another case to refer to that thing at a different time. But if we consider the two sentence-tokens of the present example—sentence-token (b) and sentence-token (c), each of which is a token of the type 'Sentence-token (b) is not true'—we will see that the subject-term in each case refers to the same sentence-token and, we may assume, both refer to that sentence-token as it is at the present time. How can it be, then, that, whereas sentence-token (c) is true, sentence-token (b) is not true?"

We should say that, if a sentence-token doesn't express a state of affairs and doesn't predicate a property of anything, then it doesn't *say* anything. Shall we now add that, if a sentence-token says of itself that it isn't true, then it doesn't say anything? This formulation will hardly do. But the thought behind it can be more carefully expressed.

Let us say: it is not possible for a sentence-token *x* to express a state of affairs that implies, with respect to *x,* that *x* is true; and it is not possible for a sentence-token *x* to express a state of affairs, that implies, with respect to *x,* that *x* is not true.[7]

Putting the matter this way, we can deal with still other attempts to construct truth-paradoxes by reference to sentence-tokens. Consider, for example, the following two tokens:

(h) *g* is true
(g) *h* is not true

We would fall into paradox if we were to say that each of these tokens is either true or false. But we should not say this. No sentence token is true or false unless it expresses a state of affairs; but if either one of the two tokens, *h* and *g,* expresses a state of affairs, then either the state of affairs will be one which implies, with respect to the sentence-token, that it is true, or the state of affairs will be one which implies, with respect to the sentence-token, that it is not true; hence, given the principle we have formulated above, we may say that neither *h* nor *g* expresses a state of affairs; and therefore neither *h* nor *g* is true or is false.[8]

[7] How are we to define the locution, "*p* implies with respect to *x* that it is *F,*" which we have used in the formulation of our principle? We may say, first, that "*p* implies the property of being *F*" means that *p* is necessarily such that, if it obtains, then something has the property of being *F*. Then we could say that "*p* implies *x* to have the property of being *F*" means this: there is a property G that (i) only one thing can have G at a time, (ii) *p* implies the conjunction of G and the property of being *F,* and (iii) *x* has G.

[8] For somewhat different treatments of these ostensible paradoxes about sentence-tokens, see Robert L. Martin, ed., *The Paradox of the Liar* (New Haven: Yale University Press, 1970). This volume contains papers by A. R. Anderson, K. S. Donnellan, F. B. Fitch, B. C. van Fraassen, N. Garver, H. Herzberger, J. Kearns, R. L. Martin, J. L. Pollock, and B. Skyrms.

**5. PUZZLES ABOUT BELIEVING**

Can we construct versions of the Epimenides involving belief? If we take as our models the ostensible paradoxes just considered, we might ask ourselves such questions as these: "What if a man had a belief that could be expressed by saying, 'The only thing I now believe is false'? Or one that could be expressed by saying, 'Everything I now believe is false'? Or one that could be expressed by saying, 'I am expressing a belief that is false'?" We can deal with each of these questions simply by saying that there couldn't be such a man.

Albertus Magnus had suggested this version of the Epimenides: While Socrates is saying, "What Plato is saying is false," Plato is saying, "What Socrates is saying is true."[9] We might try to turn this into a paradox about believing in the following way:

"Suppose (a) that what Plato now believes is that what Socrates now believes is false, and (b) that what Socrates now believes is that what Plato now believes is true. Is what Plato now believes true or false? Assume that what Plato now believes is true. Then it follows, by (a), that what Socrates now believes is false; and from this it follows, by (b), that what Plato now believes is false—which contradicts our assumption. Assume then that what Plato now believes is false. Then it follows, by (b), that what Socrates now believes is true; and from this it follows, by (a), that what Plato now believes is true—which contradicts our assumption."

Let us note there is an ambiguity in the expression "what *x* now believes." We may take it in one of three different ways: either as (i) "everything *x* now believes," or as (ii) "the one and only one thing *x* now believes," or as (iii) "something *x* now believes." Let us consider each of these three possibilities.

(i) We replace the locution "what *x* now believes" in our statement of the problem by "everything *x* now believes," saying: "Suppose (a) that everything Plato now believes is that everything Socrates now believes is false, and (b) that everything Socrates now believes is that everything Plato now believes is true." We now say simply it is impossible for Plato to be such that everything he now believes is that everything Socrates now believes is false. He will also believe that he is thinking about what Socrates believes, and he will doubtless believe, in addition, that he, Plato, exists.

(ii) The same observation will do for that version of the problem which results from replacing "what *x* now believes" by "the one and only one thing *x* now believes." It is impossible for Plato to be such that

[9] Ernest A. Moody, *Truth and Consequence in Medieval Logic* (Amsterdam: North-Holland Publishing Company, 1953), p. 103. Compare I. M. Bochenski, *Ancient Formal Logic* (Amsterdam: North-Holland Publishing Company, 1951), pp. 100–102.

the one and only one thing he believes is that the one and only one thing Socrates believes is false.

(iii) What if we replace "what *x* now believes" by "something *x* now believes"? Then we will have: "Suppose (a) that something Plato now believes is that something Socrates now believes is false, and (b) that something Socrates now believes is that something Plato now believes is true." In this case, of course, there is no paradox.

Our three readings of the locution, "what *x* now believes," may be combined in various ways in the hope of transforming the puzzle into a genuine paradox. But it is quite certain that the project will not succeed.

Still another possibility of paradox is suggested by what might be called "the problem of the philosophical fallibilist."[10] This may be put as follows:

"Suppose there is a very good inquirer who happens to be a philosophical fallibilist. When not doing philosophy, he has been completely successful in his inquiries. All his nonphilosophical beliefs—that Socrates is mortal, that 2 and 2 are 4, that there are nine planets—are true. But he has, in addition to these true beliefs, one philosophical belief. Having read Peirce, he is a fallibilist and believes, accordingly, that some of his beliefs are false. If this latter belief—that some of his beliefs are false—is true, then *it* must be the one that is false, for all his other beliefs are true. But if *it* is false, then all of his beliefs are true and therefore it is true."

Here, too, of course, we could simply deny that there can be such a man. But now, one may wonder, is the denial altogether plausible? "Couldn't there be a man who does fine, truthwise, until he gets to philosophy, and then makes the one mistake of believing that some of his beliefs are false?" I suggest that we should deny this possibility.

Should we say, then, that if a man believes that some of his beliefs are false, then he believes that some of his beliefs other than *that* belief are false? In other words, should we say that a man cannot believe (a) that some of his beliefs are false, unless he also believes (b) that he has a belief (c) such that (c) is other than (a), and (c) is false?

What if the man has no beliefs other than belief (a) and belief (b)? In such a case, is belief (b) true or false?

Consider what follows if we assume that belief (b) is true. Then belief (c) will be false. Hence (c) will not be identical with any of the man's true beliefs. And so the only belief that there is for (c) to be is (b). But this would contradict our assumption that (b) is true.

Consider, then, what follows if we assume that belief (b) is false. In this case, the man will have no false belief other than belief (a)—namely,

10 A version of this problem was first suggested to me by Keith Lehrer.

the belief that some of his beliefs are false. And this contradicts our assumption that (b) is false.

What we should say, I suggest, is this: If a man believes (a) that some of his beliefs are false, then he also believes (d) that he has a belief which is not itself a belief about what he believes and which is false.

If this assumption about the nature of believing is true, then the problem of the philosophical fallibilist is not a genuine paradox. And it is more reasonable to suppose that this assumption is true than it is to suppose that the problem of the philosophical fallibilist *is* a genuine paradox.

It would seem, then, that there aren't any genuine paradoxes about truth.

## 6. PRAGMATISM

We now take note briefly of certain other puzzling things that some philosophers have said about truth.

Some philosophers—"pragmatists" and "instrumentalists"—have said that truth consists in a kind of satisfaction, and that falsity consists in a kind of dissatisfaction. What could this mean?

"Pragmatism" and "instrumentalism" are versions of a theory concerning the nature of *believing*. And if this theory about the nature of believing is true, then the truth of a belief *is* a kind of satisfaction, and the falsity of a belief, a kind of dissatisfaction. The theory could be spelled out this way. (i) To *believe* or *accept* a certain state of affairs is to be prepared for, or set for, the occurrence of that state of affairs. (ii) To be prepared for, or set for, the occurrence of a given state of affairs is to be in a state that will be "fulfilled" or "satisfied" if, and only if, that state of affairs occurs, and "disrupted" or "disequilibrated" if, and only if, that state of affairs does not occur. (iii) The belief that the state of affairs will occur is *true* if, and only if, the state of affairs does occur. And therefore (iv) the belief will lead to satisfaction if, and only if, it is true, and to dissatisfaction if, and only if, it is false.

Thus, William James said, in effect, that if a man believes that there are tigers in India, then he is prepared, or set, for tigers being in India. And if the man is so prepared or set, James continued, then he is in a state which is such that, if he were to go to India, then he would be disrupted, disequilibrated, or surprised if, and only if, there were *no* tigers there, and he would be fulfilled or satisfied if, and only if, there *were* tigers there. Hence, on this theory of the nature of believing, the man's belief is true if, and only if (should he go to India), it is one that would produce fulfillment or satisfaction, and false if, and only if (should he go to India), it is one that would produce disruption, disequilibration, or surprise. Therefore, the theory allows us to say both that there is a sense in which truth consists in "satisfaction" and falsity in "dissatisfaction," and also, as James pointed out, that a true belief is one that "corresponds with the facts."[11] But the theory of believing from which this theory is derived would seem itself to be false.

The basic difficulty is not, as is often supposed, that the requisite concepts of satisfaction and dissatisfaction are unclear. Rather, we cannot say, of any particular belief, that that particular belief will lead to satisfaction if, and only if, it is true, or that it will lead to dissatisfaction if, and only if, it is false. The satisfactions or dissatisfactions to which the man's belief may lead (however sympathetically we interpret these terms "satisfaction" and "dissatisfaction") will be a function, in part, of his *other* beliefs. And these other beliefs may combine with a true belief to produce dissatisfaction, or with a false belief, to produce satisfaction. Thus, the belief that there are tigers in India, even if it is true, need not lead to satisfaction (the man may encounter tigers, but mistakenly think that they are lions or that he is not in India) and it may even lead to dissatisfaction (he goes to Syria, finds no tigers, and mistakenly believes that he is in India). The false proposition in our formulation of "pragmatism" above would seem to be proposition (ii).

Other more refined versions of "pragmatism" and "instrumentalism" seem to be subject to similar difficulties. I would say, therefore, that there is no clear sense in which truth can be said to consist in "satisfaction," and falsity, in "dissatisfaction."

## 7. THE TRUE AND THE EVIDENT

Our definition of "true belief" could be said to formulate the *conditions of truth* for a belief: It tells us that the acceptance of a given state of affairs is true, just on condition that that state of affairs does occur. Hence, to give the truth conditions for any belief, it is sufficient merely to express or formulate that belief. *Conditions of truth,* therefore, must be distinguished from *criteria of evidence.*

Clearly, a belief may be a belief in what is true without being a belief in what is evident. And we have also seen that a belief may be a belief in what is evident without being a belief in what is true.

In the case of what we have called the "directly evident," conditions of truth and criteria of evidence may be said to coincide. If it is evident to a man that he thinks he sees a horse, then he does think he sees a

11 James's clearest statements are in Lecture VI of *Pragmatism* (New York: David McKay Co., Inc.. 1907) and in Chapter 2 ("The Tigers in India") of *The Meaning of Truth* (New York: David McKay, Inc., 1909). Cf. John Dewey, *Logic: The Theory of Inquiry* (New York: Holt, Rinehart & Winston, Inc., 1938).

horse; and if he does think he sees a horse, then it is evident to him that he thinks he sees a horse. But in the case of other beliefs, conditions of truth and criteria of evidence do not seem to coincide. If there are criteria for saying, with respect to the belief that it rained yesterday or the belief that it will rain tomorrow, that the belief is a belief in what is now evident, or that it is one for which we now have adequate evidence, these criteria do not themselves include the fact (if it is a fact) that it did rain yesterday or that it will rain tomorrow. Hence, if we are not to be skeptics, and if we are not to restrict the evident to what is directly evident, we must face the possibility that a belief may be a belief in what is evident, or a belief for which we have adequate evidence, and, at the same time, be a belief in what is false.

But what is the good of evidence if that which is evident may also be false?[12] Is there anything we can do to secure a connection between the true and the evident? Here we have the kind of question that leads philosophers to construct "theories of reality." Consider the following three steps we might take.

1. We could begin by replacing our definition of "true belief" with one that defines the true in terms of the evident. For example, we could say, if a man accepts a given state of affairs, then, what he believes is *true,* provided it would be *evident* to a being such that, for every state of affairs, either it is evident to that being that that state of affairs occurs, or it is evident to him that that state of affairs does not occur.[13]

But this new definition of "true belief" lacks something that our earlier definition provided. Our earlier definition enabled us to say that if a man believes truly that Socrates is mortal, then it is a *fact* that Socrates is mortal. (For if he believes truly that Socrates is mortal, then the state of affairs which is Socrates being mortal is one that obtains; and a *fact,* we said, is a state of affairs that obtains.) Therefore, we were able to say that a true belief is one that "corresponds with the facts." But our new definition, as it stands, provides no guarantee that if a man believes truly that Socrates is mortal, then it is a fact that Socrates is mortal. Hence, if we define truth in this way, we may no longer be sure that our true beliefs "correspond with the facts."

12 "If you place the nature of truth in one sort of character and its test in something quite different, you are pretty certain, sooner or later, to find the two falling apart." Brand Blanshard, *The Nature of Thought,* II (London: George Allen & Unwin, 1939), p. 268.

13 "Truth pertains to the judgment of the person . . . who judges about a thing in the way in which anyone whose judgments were *evident* would judge about the thing; hence it pertains to the judgment of one who asserts what the person whose judgments are *evident* would also assert." Franz Brentano, *The True and the Evident* (London: Routledge & Kegan Paul, 1966), p. 122.

2. To obtain the needed assurance, we may be tempted to take a second step—a step into metaphysics. For we could now add a theory about the nature of "the facts" by saying that Socrates *is* mortal provided that, for a being of the sort envisaged in the new definition of "true belief," the belief that Socrates is mortal is one that would be *evident*. That is to say, Socrates *is* mortal provided that these conditions hold: Any being such that, for every state of affairs, either it is evident to him that that state of affairs occurs, or it is evident to him that that state of affairs does not occur, would be a being for whom it would be evident that Socrates is mortal. In this case, we could say not only that if it is evident to such a being that Socrates is mortal, then Socrates is mortal, but also, that if it is true that Socrates is mortal, then Socrates is mortal. And thus, we would arrive at a theory of reality—a theory that has taken various forms in the history of philosophy—that could be summarized by saying: The being who judges with evidence is "the measure of all things."[14]

But how are we to assure ourselves that a belief that is evident to *us* is one that would also be evident to a being for whom all truths are evident? Our metaphysician would have us take one more step.

3. We will now be asked to assume not only that there is such a being, a being for whom all truths are evident, but also, that each of us is identical with that being, and therefore, with each other. This, in its essentials, is what I take to be the theory of reality underlying what philosophers in the idealistic tradition have called the "coherence theory of truth."[15]

Such a theory is a very high price to pay for the desired connection

[14] Considerations such as these led Charles Sanders Peirce to conclude that "the reality of that which is real does depend on the real fact that investigation is destined to lead, at last, if continued long enough, to a belief in it"; *Collected Papers*, Vol. V (Cambridge: Harvard University Press, 1934), 5.408 (cf. 5.358*n*, 5.494, 5.565). Franz Brentano's theory (see his *The True and the Evident*) may be interpreted in a similar way, and perhaps, too, the doctrine of the stoics, who held that a "real object is one that is capable of giving rise to an apprehensive presentation"; quoted by Sextus Empiricus, *Outlines of Pyrrhonism*, Book III, in Vol. I of *Sextus Empiricus*, The Loeb Classical Library (Cambridge: Harvard University Press, 1933), p. 487.

[15] Among the clearest statements of the theory are: H. H. Joachim, *The Nature of Truth* (New York: Oxford University Press, 1906) and *Logical Studies* (New York: Oxford University Press, 1948), especially Chapter 3; Brand Blanshard, *The Nature of Thought*. The three steps I have set forth oversimplify the theory considerably; the identity asserted in the final step, for example, is usually qualified in some way or other, making the thesis somewhat difficult to grasp. "Coherence theory of truth" is also used to designate any theory which attempts to define the truth of a proposition in terms merely of the relations that the proposition bears to other propositions. Nicholas Rescher develops such a theory in *The Coherence Theory of Truth* (Oxford: The Clarendon Press, 1973); his theory, which cannot be adequately summarized here, does not presuppose a metaphysics of the sort referred to above.

between the true and the evident (though it is also thought to contribute toward the solution of certain metaphysical problems). It conflicts, moreover, with Aristotle's basic insight: "It is not because we think truly that you are pale, that you *are* pale; it is because you *are* pale that we who say this have the truth."[16] I cannot feel, therefore, that it is reasonable for anyone to accept the theory. But if we reject the theory, we must find some other way of dealing with the problems it was designed to solve.

16 *Metaphysics*, 1051b.

## CHAPTER SIX

# Knowledge

### 1. A PROBLEM FOR THE TRADITIONAL CONCEPTION OF KNOWLEDGE

According to the traditional or classical conception of knowledge, three conditions must obtain if a man knows a proposition to be true. First, the proposition must be true; second, the man must accept it; and third, the proposition must be one which, for him, is evident.[1] Hence the classical definition of knowledge may be put this way:

*S* knows that *h* is true =Df *h* is true, *S* accepts *h*, and *h* is evident for *S*.

The third clause, "*h* is evident for *S*," is sometimes expressed by saying "*h* is justified for *S*" or "*S* is justified in accepting *h*." (But we will use "evident" in place of "justified." For "justified" may also be taken to mean the same as "reasonable," or even "acceptable," and when it is

[1] Some philosophers have suggested that a proposition might be known without being accepted. For criticisms of this suggestion, see Keith Lehrer, *Knowledge* (Oxford: The Clarendon Press, 1974), Chapter 3; and D. W. Armstrong, *Belief, Truth and Knowledge* (Cambridge: Cambridge University Press, 1973), pp. 137–149.

taken in either of these ways it is not restrictive enough to be adequate to the traditional conception of knowledge.)

In countenancing the possibility that a proposition *e* may *inductively,* or *nondemonstratively,* confer evidence upon a proposition *h,* we have also countenanced the possibility that in such a case *e* is true and *h* is false. In other words, for all we know, some of the propositions that are evident to us are also false. But if this is possible, then the traditional definition must be modified.

To be sure, the definition tells us that an evident proposition is not known unless it is also true. But if it is possible for some propositions to be both evident and false, then, as we shall see, it is also possible for a person *S* to accept a true and evident proposition without thereby *knowing* that that proposition is true. This means that it is possible to satisfy the terms of the traditional definition of "*S* knows that *h* is true" even though, as a matter of fact, *S* does not know that *h* is true. Hence it would seem to be necessary to add a fourth condition to the traditional definition.

This problem for the traditional definition of knowledge was first noted by Edmund L. Gettier in a paper entitled, "Is Justified True Belief Knowledge?" first published in 1963.[2] The problem has since become known, appropriately, as "the Gettier problem." And it is also called "the problem of the fourth condition," since it leads one to ask: "Is there some suitable fourth condition which may be added to the three that are set forth in the traditional definition of knowledge?"

Gettier noted that the following situation, among others, is counter to the traditional definition of knowledge:

> Let us suppose that Smith has strong evidence for the following proposition.
>
> (f) Jones owns a Ford.
>
> Smith's evidence might be that Jones has at all times in the past within Smith's memory owned a car, and always a Ford, and that Jones has just offered Smith a ride while driving a Ford. Let us imagine, now, that Smith has another friend, Brown, of whose whereabouts he is totally ignorant. Smith selects three place-names quite at random, and constructs the following three propositions:
>
> (g) Either Jones owns a Ford, or Brown is in Boston;
>
> (h) Either Jones owns a Ford, or Brown is in Barcelona;
>
> (i) Either Jones owns a Ford, or Brown is in Brest-Litovsk.
>
> Each of these propositions is entailed by (f). Imagine that Smith realized the entailment of each of these propositions he has constructed by (f), and proceeds to accept (g), (h), and (i) on the basis of (f). Smith has correctly inferred (g), (h), and (i) from a proposition for which he has strong evidence. Smith is therefore completely justified in believing each of these three propositions. Smith, of course, has no idea where Brown is.

[2] Edmund L. Gettier, "Is Justified True Belief Knowledge?" *Analysis,* 23 (1963), 121–123.

> But imagine now that two further conditions hold. First, Jones does *not* own a Ford, but is at present driving a rented car. And second, by the sheerest coincidence, and entirely unknown to Smith, the place mentioned in proposition (h) happens really to be the place where Brown is. If these two conditions hold, then Smith does *not* know that (h) is true, even though (*i*) (h) is true, (*ii*) Smith does believe that (h) is true, and (*iii*) Smith is justified in believing that (h) is true.[3]

Hence, Gettier concludes, the traditional definition of knowledge does not give us a *sufficient* reason for saying that someone knows a given proposition to be true. For a man and a proposition—the Smith and the (h) of Gettier's example—could satisfy the conditions set forth in the traditional definition even though the man does *not* know the proposition to be true.

Gettier was the first philosopher to see that the traditional definition of knowledge is thus inadequate. Since the publication of his now classic paper in 1963, many other counter-examples to the traditional definition have been formulated, most of them not different in principle from the one just cited, though others of them—to be considered below—raising problems of a somewhat different sort. Once Gettier had pointed out the inadequacy of the traditional definition, it then became apparent that certain other cases which had puzzled earlier philosophers could also have been used to show that the traditional definition requires modification. We will mention two of these, one suggested by A. Meinong in 1906, the other by Bertrand Russell in 1948.

Meinong considers an Austrian garden where there is an Aeolian harp made to whistle in the wind and thereby keep the birds away. "Assume now," he says, "that someone who has lived in the vicinity of such an apparatus has become hard of hearing in the course of time and has developed a tendency to have auditory hallucinations. It could easily happen that he hallucinates the familiar sounds of the Aeolian harp at the very moment at which these sounds are actually to be heard."[4] If this were to happen, then, given the theory of perception set forth in the present work, one might say that the man had a true and evident belief to the effect that the harp was then sounding. But it hardly would be true to say that he thereby *knew* that the harp was then sounding.

Russell wrote: "It is very easy to give examples of true beliefs that are not knowledge. There is the man who looks at a clock which is not

[3] Ibid., pp. 122–123.

[4] A. Meinong, *Über die Erfahrungsgrundlagen unseres Wissens* (Berlin: Julius Springer, 1906), pp. 30–31. Meinong constructs another example, involving a man who is disturbed by a ringing in his ears at a time when, as luck would have it, someone happens to be ringing the doorbell. The two examples may be found in Volume V of the Meinong *Gesamtausgabe* (Graz: Akademische Druck- und Verlagsanstalt, 1973), ed. Roderick M. Chisholm, pp. 398–399, 619.

going, though he thinks it is, and who happens to look at it the moment when it is right; this man acquires a true belief as to the time of day, but cannot be said to have knowledge. There is the man who believes, truly, that the last name of the Prime Minister in 1906 began with a B, but who believes this because he thinks that Balfour was Prime Minister then, whereas it was Campbell Bannerman."[5] (The second man may be compared with those supporters of Senator McGovern who believed, in 1972, that Nixon's successor would be a man whose first name begins with G.) If we add, in these cases, that the true propositions in question are also evident, then we have further counter-examples to the traditional definition of knowledge.

Still another example would be this. A man *takes* there to be a sheep in the field and does so under conditions which are such that, when a man *does* thus take there to be a sheep in the field, then it is *evident* to him that there is a sheep in the field. The man, however, has mistaken a dog for a sheep and so what he sees is not a sheep at all. Nevertheless, unsuspected by the man, there *is* a sheep in another part of the field. Hence, the proposition that there is a sheep in the field will be one that is both true and evident and it will also be one that the man accepts. But the situation does not warrant our saying that the man *knows* that there is a sheep in the field.

It may be noted that one feature that is common to all these examples is the following. The true proposition which constitutes a counter-example to the traditional definition of knowledge is a proposition for which the man has only inductive or nondemonstrative evidence. It is made evident for him by propositions that do not entail it. One may be tempted to say, therefore, that no such proposition can be known to be true. But, as we have seen, unless we are to restrict the things that can be said to be known to those things that are directly evident, then we must be prepared to face the possibility that some of the things we know are not demonstratively evident. And we have agreed that our knowledge does extend beyond the directly evident.

People do know such things as that Jones owns a Ford—where the evidence does not significantly differ in content from the kind of evidence that Gettier described.

Some philosophers have attempted to deal with the problem of the fourth condition merely by stipulating that no proposition $e$ confers evidence upon any proposition $h$ unless $e$ entails $h$. These philosophers have not realized, apparently, that any such stipulation restricts our knowledge to what we have called the directly evident.

5 Bertrand Russell, *Human Knowledge: Its Scope and Limits* (New York: Simon and Schuster, 1948), p. 155.

Other philosophers, after reflection upon this problem, have despaired of providing any definition of knowledge at all and have suggested that perhaps the best we can do is merely to formulate certain necessary conditions of certain types of knowledge.[6]

But we will attempt to repair the traditional definition of knowledge.

## 2. A DIAGNOSIS

Many different repairs have been suggested, but unfortunately there is no consensus as to whether any of them has been successful. Many of them are very difficult to understand, for they go considerably beyond the store of concepts we have permitted ourselves in the present work.[7] We will not attempt to evaluate the various suggestions that have been made, but will simply ask whether the traditional definition can be repaired within the general scheme of concepts that has been set forth here.

Let us now consider two further concepts: that of one proposition being a *basis* for another, and that of one proposition being such that it *confers evidence* upon another. Each of these two concepts may be defined in terms of the concepts that have already been introduced. The concept of one proposition being a *basis* for another may be defined this way:

D6.1 *e* is a *basis* of *h* for *S* =Df *e* is self-presenting for *S;* and necessarily, if *e* is self-presenting for *S*, then *h* is evident for *S*.

[6] Compare Alvin I. Goldman, "A Causal Theory of Knowing," *Journal of Philosophy*, LXIV (1967), 357–372. Goldman here suggests that, if *S* knows a contingent proposition *h*, then *S* has a justified true belief to the effect that *h* is causally connected with his acceptance of *h*. But Goldman does not offer this suggestion as an analysis or definition of knowing. And it is obvious that knowledge cannot be defined in this way, since (i) some of the propositions we know are not contingent propositions and (ii) it is possible to have a justified true belief about the causal connection between *h* and one's acceptance of *h*, without thereby having knowledge of that causal connection.

[7] Some of these attempts are published in Michael D. Roth and Leon Galis, *Knowing: Essays in the Analysis of Knowledge* (New York: Random House, 1970). Compare also: Keith Lehrer and Thomas Paxson, "Knowledge: Undefeated Justified True Belief," *Journal of Philosophy*, LXVI (1969), 225–237; Fred Dretske, "Conclusive Reasons," *Australasian Journal of Philosophy*, 49 (1971), 1–22; Peter D. Klein, "A Proposed Definition of Propositional Knowledge," *Journal of Philosophy*, LXIII (1971), 471–482; Marshall Swain, "Knowledge, Causality, and Justification," *Journal of Philosophy*, LXIX (1972), 291–300; Bredo C. Johnsen, "Knowledge," *Philosophical Studies*, XXV (1974), 273–382; John L. Pollock, *Knowledge and Justification* (Princeton: Princeton University Press, 1974); Keith Lehrer, *Knowledge* (Oxford: The Clarendon Press, 1974); Marshall Swain, "Epistemic Defeasibility," *American Philosophical Quarterly*, XI (1974), 15–25; and Ernest Sosa, "How Do You Know?" *American Philosophical Quarterly*, XI (1974), 113–122.

We could also express the definiendum by saying "*e* is a basis of *h* being evident for *S*." (It should be noted that the concept of *basis,* as thus defined, is restricted to what is self-presenting. And so a directly evident proposition that is not self-presenting will not constitute a basis, in the present sense of the term.) Given this concept of a basis, we may now explicate the relation of *conferring evidence* in the following way:

D6.2 *e confers evidence* upon *h* for *S* =Df *e* is evident for *S;* and every *b* such that *b* is a basis of *e* for *S* is a basis of *h* for *S*.

(In place of "*e* confers evidence upon *h* for *S*," we may also say "*e* makes *h* evident for *S*.") We may now say that *e deductively* confers evidence on *h* provided that *e* confers evidence on *h* and also logically implies *h*. But if *e* confers evidence on *h* and does not logically imply *h,* then *e inductively* confers evidence on *h*.

We may note that, if *e* is a basis of *h* for *S,* then *e* may also be said to confer evidence upon *h* for *S*.

Let us now return to the example we have quoted from Gettier. What we say about this can also be said *mutatis mutandis* about the other examples that have been mentioned. (i) There is a set of propositions *e* such that *e* inductively confers evidence for Smith upon the false proposition *f* that Jones owns a Ford. We suppose that *e* contains such propositions as these: "Jones has at all times in the past within Smith's memory owned a car, and always a Ford," "Jones keeps a Ford in his garage," "Jones has just offered Smith a ride while driving a Ford," and various other propositions of this same sort.[8] (ii) Smith accepts the false but evident *f* ("Jones owns a Ford"). (iii) We assume that *f* deductively confers evidence upon the disjunctive proposition *h* that either Jones owns a Ford or Brown is in Barcelona. And we suppose that, as luck would have it and entirely unsuspected by Smith, Brown *is* in Barcelona. Therefore, *h* ("Either Jones owns a Ford or Brown is in Barcelona") is true. And (iv) Smith, who sees that *f,* which he believes to be true, entails *h,* also believes that *h* is true. Hence the proposition "Either

[8] Some authors, I believe, have been misled in two respects by Gettier's example: (1) He has used "justify" where I have used "confer evidence upon." But "*e* justifies *h* for *S*" may be taken in a sense which does not imply "*e* confers evidence upon *h* for *S*." If one takes "justifies" in any such weaker sense, the example given would not be counter to the traditional definition of knowledge; it is essential that *e* confer evidence upon *h*. (2) The two propositions which Gettier cites as members of *e* ("Jones has at all times in the past within Smith's memory owned a car and always a Ford" and "Jones has just offered Smith a ride while driving a Ford") are not themselves sufficient to confer evidence for Smith upon the false proposition *f* ("Jones owns a Ford"). At the most they justify *f* only in the weaker sense of making *f* reasonable, or acceptable. In discussing the example, however, we will imagine that *e* contains still other propositions and that it does confer evidence upon *f* for Smith.

Jones owns a Ford or Brown is in Barcelona" is a proposition which is such that: it is true, Smith believes that it is true, and it is evident for Smith. But our description of the situation does not warrant our saying that Smith knows it to be true.

What has gone wrong?

Is it that the evidence *e* that Smith has for *h* also confers evidence upon a false proposition? This isn't quite the difficulty. For we may assume that *e* itself is a proposition that *S* knows to be true; but *e* confers evidence upon a false proposition; therefore whatever confers evidence upon *e* also confers evidence upon a false proposition; and so a proposition *can* be known though what confers evidence upon it confers evidence upon a false proposition.

How, then, shall we repair the traditional definition of knowledge? Of the possibilities that first come to mind, some exclude too much and others exclude too little.

Shall we say, for example: "If a man knows a proposition *h* to be true, then *nothing* that confers evidence upon *h* for him confers evidence upon a false proposition"? This would exclude too much. Consider some proposition *k* that the Smith of Gettier's example does know to be true and suppose that Smith accepts the conjunction of *k* and *f*, where *f* is the false but evident "Jones owns a Ford." Since the conjunction, *k* and *f*, confers evidence upon *k* for Smith and also upon the false proposition *f*, the proposed qualification would require us to say that Smith does not know that *k* is true.

Should we say: "If a man knows a proposition *h* to be true, then *something* that confers evidence upon *h* for him is such as not to confer evidence upon a false proposition"? This would exclude too little. Suppose that the *h* of Gettier's example ("Jones owns a Ford or Brown is in Barcelona") does not confer evidence upon any false proposition for Smith. Then there will be something which deductively confers evidence upon *h* for Smith and which confers evidence upon no false proposition; this something could be *h* itself as well as the conjunction of *h* with various other evident propositions that do not confer evidence upon false propositions. Hence the proposed qualification would require us to say that the Smith of Gettier's example does know *h* to be true.

Have we construed "*e* confers evidence upon *h*" too broadly? We began by considering a single "*h*-evidencer"—a single set of propositions *e* which conferred evidence upon *h* for *S*. But we have seen that even our simple example involves many additional *h*-evidencers. In addition to *e* there are: *h* itself; the disjunction "*h* or *e*"; the disjunction "(*h* and *p*) or *e*," where *p* is any proposition; the disjunction "(*e* and *p*) or *h*"; the conjunction "*e* and *k*," where *k* is any other evident proposition; thus also the conjunction "*e* and *f*," where *f* is a false but evident proposition; and such disjunctions as "(*e* and *f*) or *h*" and "(*h* and *p*) or (*e* and *k*)."[9]

Though we thus seem able to construct *h*-evidencers *ad indefinitum,* some of them would seem to be parasitical upon others. If we had a way of marking off the parasitical *h*-evidencers from the nonparasitical ones, then perhaps we could repair the traditional definition of knowledge by formulating a qualification in terms merely of *S*'s nonparasitical *h*-evidencers. A nonparasitical *h*-evidencer would be one which, so to speak, did not derive any of its epistemic force from any of *S*'s other *h*-evidencers. What, then, would be an instance of such a nonparasitical *h*-evidencer?

The answer is obvious. *S*'s nonparasitical *h*-evidencers are to be found among those self-presenting propositions which are a basis for *h* being evident for *S*. Let us distinguish, then, between those self-presenting propositions which make some falsehood evident for *S* and those self-presenting propositions which do not. And then by reference to this distinction we may be able to repair the traditional definition of knowledge.

## 3. THE TRADITIONAL DEFINITION REPAIRED

To repair the traditional definition, we will single out a class of propositions which we will call "nondefectively evident."[10] If a proposition is thus nondefectively evident for our subject *S,* then it has a self-presenting basis which makes no falsehood evident for *S*. Let us say, more exactly:

D6.3 *h* is *nondefectively evident* for *S* =Df Either *h* is certain for *S,* or *h* is evident for *S* and is entailed by a conjunction of propositions each having for *S* a basis which is not a basis of any false proposition for *S*.

(It will be recalled that "*e* is a basis for *h* for *S*" abbreviates "*e* is a basis for *h* being evident for *S*.") If an evident proposition is not nondefectively evident, then, of course, it is defectively evident.

Why not say, more simply, that *h* is nondefectively evident for *S* provided only that it has a basis which is not a basis of any false proposition for *S*? This will not yet give us what we want. For consider the *e*

[9] Still other *h*-evidencers for *S* may be constructed by disjoining any of the *h*-evidencers above with certain propositions *e′* which would confer evidence upon *h* if they were themselves evident. Suppose, for example, *e′* is "Jones has just bought a car from the local Ford dealer; the Registery of Motor Vehicles and other reliable and trustworthy authorities affirm that Jones owns a Ford; etc." Then whether or not *e′* is true, and whether or not it is evident for *S,* the epistemic state of *S* may be such that such disjunctions as "*e* or *e′*" and "*h* or *e′*" also make *h* evident for him.

[10] I borrow this use of the terms "defective" and "nondefective" from Ernest Sosa.

of Gettier's example: "Jones has at all times in the past owned a car and always a Ford; Jones keeps a Ford in his garage; Jones has just offered Smith a ride while driving a Ford; . . ." This conjunctive proposition *e*, we have agreed, is one that *S* knows to be true. But *e* makes evident the false "Jones owns a Ford." Therefore, if there is a self-presenting proposition *d* such that *d* is a basis of *e* being evident for *S*, then *d* also makes a false proposition evident for *S*. And so the definition of "nondefectively evident" must be formulated in such a way that *e* will not be defective; hence the formulation in D6.3.

But let us note that *e* is a conjunction: "($e^1$) Jones has at all times in the past owned a car and always a Ford; ($e^2$) Jones keeps a Ford in his garage; ($e^3$) Jones has offered Smith a ride while driving a Ford; ($e^4$). . . ." We have said that, in conjunction, this set of propositions makes evident the false proposition *f* that Jones owns a Ford. But, we may assume, no one of these conjuncts is sufficient *by itself* to make evident for *S* that Jones owns a Ford. And, we may also assume, each of these conjuncts has a basis which is not a basis for any false proposition.

We may therefore, replace the traditional definition of knowledge by this:

D6.4 *h* is *known* by *S* =Df *h* is accepted by *S*; *h* is true; and *h* is nondefectively evident for *S*.

The *e* of Gettier's example, if our diagnosis is right, is a proposition that is known by Smith. It is true, it is believed by Smith, and it is equivalent to a conjunction of propositions each of which is nondefectively evident for Smith. But the *h* of Gettier's example—"Jones owns a Ford or Brown is in Barcelona"—is defectively evident. The only set of self-presenting propositions that makes *h* evident for Smith is one that also makes evident for Smith the false proposition *f*, that Jones owns a Ford. Therefore the repaired definition of knowledge, unlike the original traditional definition, does not require us to say of Smith that he knows *h* to be true.

The other examples we have mentioned would be treated similarly. Meinong's hallucinating gardener cannot be said to know that the Aeolian harp is sounding. To be sure, the self-presenting "I take that to be the sound of an Aeolian harp" does provide him with a basis for the true proposition that the Aeolian harp is sounding. But it also provides him with a basis for the *false* proposition "The sounds I now hear are caused by the whistling of the Aeolian harp" and therefore the proposition that the Aeolian harp is sounding is one that is defectively evident and hence not known to be true. Analogously for Russell's examples. There is a set of self-presenting propositions which provide a basis for the true proposition that the time of day is what the clock now says it is—even though the clock has long since stopped. But those propositions also provide a basis for the false proposition that one moment ago the time of day was what the clock then said it was, and therefore the proposition about the time of day is defectively evident and hence not known to be true. In the case of the man who mistakes a dog for a sheep, the true proposition "There is a sheep in the field" is made evident by the self-presenting proposition "I take there to be a sheep in the field." But this self-presenting proposition is also a basis for the false proposition "What I take to be a sheep *is* a sheep." And so "There is a sheep in the field" is defectively evident and hence not known to be true.

## 4. THE DIAGNOSIS DEFENDED

The account of knowledge that we have proposed has at least this disadvantage in common with other attempts to solve the problem of the fourth condition: it is not immediately obvious that the definition is correct. The definition is one that must be defended.

In what follows we will formulate what seem to be the most common objections to this account of knowledge and we will attempt to reply to them. For it is only by considering such objections and the possible replies to them that one can appreciate the difficulties that our problem involves.

The first objection may be put as follows:

1. "Suppose a man knows that (e) 99 percent of the balls in the urn are black and that the many drawings from the urn that are about to take place are to be random ones. This fact surely will make it evident to him that (h) most of the drawings will be of balls that are black. But suppose now that although it is true that (h) most of the drawings will be of balls that are black, it is false that (f) the next ball to be drawn will be black. The self-presenting propositions that constitute a basis for (e) and therefore also for (h) will also constitute a basis for (f). And therefore your definition will not allow you to say that the man knows (h) to be true. But surely, if he believes (h) he does know it to be true."

The reply to this objection is that, although the man's evidence (e) may well *make reasonable* for him the false proposition (f), it can hardly be said to make it *evident*. To see the difference between the epistemic status of (h) and (f) in this situation, we have only to imagine ourselves in the same epistemic situation as the man in question. We would readily grant him the right to say, "I know that most of the drawings will be black." But if he went on to say, "And what's more, I know that the next ball to be drawn will be black," our reaction would be to reply: "Either you're mistaken or else you have some evidence other than (e) that we do not have."

The objection reminds us that, if a proposition is one that is *known* to be true, then it is one that is justified, not only in the sense of being acceptable or reasonable for the man, but also in the sense of being evident.

To prepare ourselves for the second objection, let us suppose a man has adequate evidence for propositions he might express as follows:

(a) "Whenever the factory whistle blows, it is 5 P.M.";
(b) "Whenever the factory whistle blows, the bus will appear within five minutes";
(c) "The factory whistle is now blowing."

We may assume that in such a case the following will also be evident:

(d) "It is now 5 P.M."
(e) "The bus will appear within five minutes."

And let us suppose further that it is in fact 5 P.M. but that, on this particular occasion, the bus has broken down and will not appear. Referring now to this situation, one might object to our definition of knowledge in the following way:

2. "Surely (i) the man does know that *d* is true; he does know that it is 5 P.M. But (ii) *d* is made evident to him by *c*, by the fact that the factory whistle is now blowing. And so (iii) the directly evident propositions that make *c* evident for the man, and thus constitute a basis for *c*, will also be the ones that make *d* evident. But (iv) *c* also makes evident the false proposition *e*, that the bus will now appear. Hence (v) the self-presenting propositions constituting the man's basis for *d* also constitute a basis for a false proposition. Therefore (vi) your definition of knowledge would require us to say, incorrectly, that the man does not know *d* to be true, i.e., that he does not know that it is 5 P.M."

The mistakes in this reasoning lie in steps (ii) and (iii). Thus it is a mistake to say in (ii) that *d* is made evident to the man by *c*. The fact that it is now 5 P.M. is *not* made evident to him by the fact that the whistle is blowing. Rather, it is made evident for him by the conjunction of *c* and *a*—the whistle blowing taken in conjunction with the general proposition that, whenever the factory whistle blows, it is 5 P.M. And analogously for step (iii); the false proposition *e* is made evident, not by *c* alone, but by *c* and *b*. The directly evident propositions that make *d* evident for the man are those that make evident the conjunction, *a* and *c*. But those that make evident the false proposition *e* are those that make evident the conjunction, *b* and *c*. And so step (v) of the argument is false; it is not the case that the self-presenting propositions constituting the man's basis for *d* also constitute a basis for a false proposition.

We may note that the objection is based upon a fallacy that is very readily committed. One assumes that, if two propositions in conjunction make evident a third proposition, then if both propositions *are* evident, it will follow that either one of those propositions taken separately may be said to make evident that third proposition.

The third objection raises the question whether our definition of knowledge is adequate to the fact that some of our knowledge is *a priori*.

3. "The account of knowledge you have given implies that we cannot know any proposition to be true unless the proposition is based upon something that is self-presenting. Now, by your account, whatever is self-presenting is quite obviously something that is subjective and contingent. But you have said that there are certain 'eternal truths of reason' that can be known *a priori,* and you have rejected all 'psychologistic' interpretations of these truths. Such truths, obviously, cannot be based upon what is contingent and subjective. Therefore, your proposed definition of knowledge is inconsistent with your claim that we have *a priori* knowledge of certain eternal truths."

The mistake in this reasoning lies in the contention that what is self-presenting cannot provide a basis for what is *a priori*. We have said, in effect, that if you know a proposition *a priori,* then the proposition is one which you accept and which is necessarily such that, if you accept it, then it is evident for you.[11] And we have said, in D6.1, that if a proposition *e* is a *basis* of a proposition *h* for *S,* then "necessarily, if *e* is self-presenting for *S,* then *h* is evident for *S*." Putting the two accounts together, we see that what is known *a priori* can have a basis in the fact that one accepts it.

Perhaps it will be recalled, incidentally, that *a priori* knowledge was defined in Chapter 3:

D3.3 *h* is known *a priori* by *S* =Df There is an *e* such that (i) *e* is axiomatic for *S,* (ii) the proposition, *e* implies *h,* is axiomatic for *S,* and (iii) *S* accepts *h*.

We may assume that whatever is thus known *a priori* satisfies the conditions of knowledge we have set forth above.

## 5. KNOWING THAT ONE KNOWS

The definition of knowledge we have given is best understood when considered together with certain general principles pertaining to the evidence of evidence and to knowing that one knows.

Shall we say that, if a proposition is evident, then it is also evident

[11] A more exact statement may be found in Chapter 3; see in particular, the first four definitions in that chapter.

that it is evident? Or that, if a proposition is evident, then it is evident that it is known?[12]

We have emphasized that a proposition cannot be evident to a person unless the person understands the proposition. Now it is possible that there is a person who does not yet have the concept of evidence or of knowledge, but for whom, all the same, a certain proposition is known. Such a person, then, would be one for whom it could not be evident that anything is known or evident. Therefore a proposition may be evident without it being evident that it is evident, and a proposition may be known without it being known that it is known.[13]

Shall we say, then, that if a proposition is evident, and if one asks oneself whether it is evident, *then* it is evident that the proposition is evident? This is less objectionable, for one cannot ask oneself such a question unless one *does* have the concept of a proposition being evident. But let us say more simply that, if a proposition is evident and if one *considers* the proposition, then it is evident that the proposition is evident:

(K1) If *S* considers the proposition that he knows that *p*, and if it is evident to *S* that *p*, then it is evident to *S* that he knows that *p*.

(This principle is a schema in which the letter "*p*" may be replaced by any declarative English sentence.) We may assume that, if a proposition is evident to *S*, and if he considers it, then he also accepts it.

Evidence to the effect that one knows a given proposition may be defective. But we may assume that, in such a case, the evidence for the proposition is also defective. In other words, propositions about what one knows cannot be the sole propositions that are defectively evident:

(K2) If it is evident to *S* that he knows that *p*, and if *S* does not know that *p*, then there is a false proposition which is evident for *S* and which neither implies nor is implied by the proposition that *p*.

According to K2, then, if the proposition that he knows that *p* is defectively evident for *S*, then some *other* proposition, logically independent of *p*, is also defectively evident for *S*.

We should also say that, if it is evident to *S* that he knows a certain

[12] Compare John Pollock: "Whenever *h* is evident for a person, then it is also evident for him that he knows *h*." From "Chisholm's Definition of Knowledge," *Philosophical Studies*, XIX (1968), 72–76; the quotation is on p. 74.

[13] This point is made by Arthur Danto in "On Knowing That We Know," in *Epistemology: New Essays in the Theory of Knowledge*, ed. Avrum Stroll (New York: Harper & Row, 1967), pp. 32–53. But contrast Brentano, who held that the fact that a proposition is evident for a person *S* is sufficient to give *S* the concept of a proposition being evident; see *The True and the Evident* (London: Routledge & Kegan Paul, 1966), p. 125.

proposition, then it is also evident to *S* that there is no true proposition which would defeat or override the evidence he has for that proposition. But in order to formulate this principle, we should introduce a definition of the expression, "evidence *S* has for *h*."[14] This expression might be explicated in the following way:

D6.5 *e* is evidence *S* has for *h* =Df Either (i) *e* is identical with *h* and is directly evident or *a priori* for *S* or (ii) *e* does not imply *h* but confers evidence upon *h* for *S*.

And now we may say:

(K3) If it is evident to *S* that he knows that *p*, then it is evident to *S* that the result of adding any true proposition to his evidence for *p* either implies *p* or would confer evidence upon *p*.

This principle tells us, in effect, that if it is evident to a man that he knows that *p*, then, it is evident to him that there is no true proposition that could disturb the case he has for *p*. It might also be put by saying that, if it is evident to a man that he knows that *p*, then he has the right to be sure that this knowledge cannot be lost simply as the result of learning something new.

Principle K3 should be contrasted with a stronger principle, which has been accepted by some philosophers. The stronger principle says that, if it is evident to a man that he knows that *p*, then *in fact* there is no true proposition that could disturb the case he has for *p*. Thus, where K3 tells us merely that the man has a *right to be sure that* his knowledge cannot be lost simply as the result of learning something new, the stronger principle says that in fact his knowledge *will not* be lost simply as the result of learning something new.[15]

If K3 is true, then we may say that, if it is evident for *S* that he knows that *p*, then it is evident for *S* that nothing that anyone else knows could disturb the case that he has for *h*. This fact has been said to express the "social aspect" of knowledge.[16] We could agree with Harman that, in a

[14] It would not do to say simply that if *e* confers evidence upon *h* for *S*, then *e* is evidence *S* has for *h*. For given our definition of "*e* confers evidence upon *h* for *S*" (D6.2), *h* itself, if it is evident, will be one of the propositions that confers evidence upon *h* for *S*; so, too, for the conjunction of *h* and any other proposition that is evident for *S*. But except in the case of the self-presenting and the axiomatic, we should not say that a proposition is evidence for itself.

[15] Risto Hilpinen says, "Knowledge cannot be 'lost' simply as a result of learning something new," and refers to this stronger thesis as the *extendability thesis*. See his "Knowledge and Justification," *Ajatus: Yearbook of the Philosophical Society of Finland*, XXXIII (1971), 7–39; the thesis is on p. 25. Compare J. Hintikka, *Knowledge and Belief* (Ithaca: Cornell University Press, 1962), pp. 20–21.

[16] Compare Ernest Sosa, "The Analysis of 'Knowledge That *P*,' " *Analysis*, XXV

certain sense, "evidence that one does not possess" is relevant to the question whether or not one knows.[17]

Shall we now say that, if a person knows a certain proposition, then, *ipso facto,* he knows that he knows it? This principle has been affirmed by many philosophers.[18] But since one may know before one has the concept of what it is to know, it would seem more reasonable to affirm a qualified version of the principle. Let us say:

(K4) If *S* considers the proposition that he knows that *p,* and if he does know that *p,* then he knows that he knows that *p.*

This principle is suggested by H. A. Prichard: ". . . whenever we know something, we either do, or at least can, by reflecting, directly know that we are knowing it."[19]

## 6. THE RIGHT TO BE SURE

If a man *knows* that a proposition is true, then he is justified in believing that there is no truth that could disturb the case that he has for that proposition. Scholastic philosophers have put this point by saying that, if a man knows a proposition to be true, then his grounds for the proposition are "sufficient to exclude all prudent fear of error"; the man need not fear that anything will show the proposition to be false.[20] A. J. Ayer has said, similarly, that knowledge implies "having the right to be sure."[21]

But doesn't this lead to a kind of dogmatism and infallibilism that is inconsistent with the spirit of free inquiry? Thus John Dewey said that, since knowledge gives us the right to be sure, it "terminates inquiry": if

---

(1964), 1–8; Gilbert Harman, "Knowledge, Inference, and Explanation," *American Philosophical Quarterly,* V (1968), 164–173.

17 Gilbert Harman, *Thought* (Princeton: Princeton University Press, 1973), pp. 142–154.

18 See the references on pp. 107–109 of Hintikka's *Knowledge and Belief;* Hintikka also affirms a version of this principle. Compare: E. J. Lemmon, "If I Know, Do I Know That I Know?" in *Epistemology: New Essays in the Theory of Knowledge,* ed. Avrum Stroll (New York: Harper & Row, 1967), pp. 54–82; Carl Ginet, "What Must Be Added to Knowing to Obtain Knowing that One Knows," *Synthese,* XXI (1970), 163–186; and Risto Hilpinen, "Knowing that One Knows and the Classical Definition of Knowledge," *Synthese,* XXI (1970), 109–132.

19 H. A. Prichard, *Knowledge and Perception* (Oxford: The Clarendon Press, 1950), p. 86.

20 Compare P. Coffey, *Epistemology,* Vol. I (London: Longmans, Green and Co., 1917), Chapter 1; and D. J. Mercier, *Criteriologie Générale,* 8th ed. (Louvain: Institut Supérieur de Philosophie, 1923), pp. 6–15.

21 A. J. Ayer, *The Problem of Knowledge* (Middlesex: Penguin Books Ltd., 1956), p. 35.

a man *knows* a proposition to be true, then, so far as *that* proposition is concerned, he may regard his inquiry as closed. "That which satisfactorily terminates inquiry is, by definition, knowledge; it is knowledge because it *is* the appropriate close of inquiry."[22] In other words, if we know, we need not inquire any further and there is no need for us to consider any evidence indicating that we might be mistaken in thinking that we know. But Dewey took this fact to show, not that we ever do thus have the right to terminate inquiry, but rather that there is very little, if anything, that we ever really know.[23]

Are we mistaken, then, in saying that there *are* things that we know? Or have we misconceived the nature of knowing?

The problem has been formulated by Harman in the following way: " 'If I know that *h* is true, I know that any evidence against *h* is evidence against something that is true; so I know that such evidence is misleading. But I should disregard evidence that I know is misleading. So, once I know that *h* is true, I am in a position to disregard any further evidence that seems to tell against *h*.' This is paradoxical, because I am never in a position simply to disregard any future evidence even though I do know a great many different things."[24]

We should note that there is a certain ambiguity in the expression "right to be sure." For in saying that a man has the "right to be sure" of a certain proposition, we may be saying one or the other of two quite different things.

In saying that a man has the "right to be sure" of a given proposition, one *could* mean that the man has the right to "terminate inquiry" and to disregard any future evidence that seems to tell against the proposition. But if *this* is the right that knowing confers, then we know next to nothing about the things around us; for surely the reasonable man never has the right to close his mind and disregard all future evidence. And so in this sense of "right to be sure," it would be a mistake to say both that knowledge confers this right and that reasonable men do know most of the things they think they know.

But there is another sense of "right to be sure." And if we take the expression in this second sense, then we can say both that knowledge confers this right and that we do know the things that we have said that we know. This second sense pertains to the application of the theory of probability.

We may say with Bishop Butler that probability is or ought to be "the

22 John Dewey, *Logic: The Theory of Inquiry* (New York: Henry Holt & Co., 1938), p. 8.

23 Compare Lehrer, *Knowledge,* pp. 78ff.

24 Gilbert Harman, *Thought,* p. 148. Harman notes that, in formulating this problem, he is indebted to Saul Kripke.

very guide of life."[25] In making our plans and our decisions we should be guided in part by probabilities. But by *what* probabilities? Probability is a relation between propositions; and one and the same proposition may have different probabilities in relation to different propositions. Of these indefinitely many probabilities that a given proposition may have, *which* is the one that should guide us when we make a decision with respect to that proposition? The answer is that we should be guided by the *absolute* probability of the proposition—the probability that the proposition has in relation to what we know.[26]

What, then, is the "right to be sure" that is conferred by knowledge? If we *know* that a certain proposition is true, then we have the right to use that proposition, along with the other things we know, in calculating probabilities. We have a right to be sure that, to the extent that we rely on *that* proposition as a basis for calculating the probabilities of other propositions, our decisions will be reasonable ones.

But to say that we have this right to be sure is not to say that we have the right to terminate inquiry or to disregard any future evidence that seems to tell against what it is that we are now justified in thinking that we know. For it is one thing to have the right to use a certain proposition in calculating probabilities; it is another thing to have the right to close one's mind to the possibility that one might be wrong.

[25] In the Introduction to the *Analogy;* see *The Whole Works of Bishop Butler, LL.D.* (London: Thomas Tegg, 1839), p. xxxiv.

[26] The concept of absolute probability is closely related to the concept of confirmation that we have discussed. Thus we could say that, in the absolute sense, a proposition *h* is *more probable than not* for a given subject *S* provided these conditions hold: there is a proposition *e* such that (i) *e* is known by *S,* (ii) *e* tends to confirm *h,* and (iii) there is no *i* such that *i* is known by *S* and the conjunction *e* and *i* does not tend to confirm *h.* (We may assume that any proposition that is thus more probable than not is one that has some presumption in its favor.) The term "absolute probability," in the present sense, was used by Bernard Bolzano; see his *Theory of Science,* ed. Rolf George (Oxford: Basil Blackwell, 1972), pp. 359–365. Compare J. M. Keynes, *A Treatise on Probability* (London: Macmillan, 1952), pp. 3–19, 307–323; and Rudolf Carnap, *Logical Foundations of Probability* (Chicago: University of Chicago Press, 1950), pp. 19–51, 161–252.

## CHAPTER SEVEN

# The Problem of the Criterion

**1. INTRODUCTION** There are many areas of knowledge, or possible areas of knowledge, that we have not touched upon. What of our knowledge of ethics and morality—our knowledge of what is good and what is bad, and of what is right and what is wrong? What of our knowledge of "other minds"—our knowledge of the thoughts, beliefs, and feelings of other people? And what of that knowledge of God and "the Holy" which some people, at least in some of their moods, believe to be readily accessible to us?

We saw, in discussing the directly evident, that the problems involved in asking, "What justification can a man have for thinking there is a cat on the roof?" become extraordinarily intricate and difficult. Those involved in these other areas—ethics and morality, other people, and God and the Holy—are not likely to be any simpler. We will not attempt to consider each of them in detail. But we will consider certain general features which are common to all of these questions about knowledge. In so doing, we may throw some light upon the controversies that have divided philosophers. And in consequence, I think, we may be able to understand somewhat more adequately the nature of the problems that have concerned us up to now.

**2. TWO QUESTIONS** Let us consider once again the general nature of the problems of epistemology.

We may distinguish two very general questions. These are, "*What* do we know?" and "How are we to decide, in any particular case, *whether* we know?" The first of these may also be put by asking, "What is the *extent* of our knowledge?" and the second, by asking, "What are the *criteria* of knowing?"

If we know the answer to either one of these questions, then perhaps we may devise a procedure that will enable us to answer the other. If we can specify the criteria of knowledge, we may have a way of deciding how far our knowledge extends. Or if we know how far it does extend, and are able to say what the things are that we know, then we may be able to formulate criteria enabling us to mark off the things that we do know from those that we do not.

But if we do not have the answer to the first question, then, it would seem, we have no way of answering the second. And if we do not have the answer to the second, then, it would seem, we have no way of answering the first.

It is characteristic of "empiricism" (but not only of "empiricism") to assume that we have an answer to the second of these two questions and then to attempt to answer the first on the basis of the answer to the second. *Experience,* in one or another of its various senses, is said to provide us with the marks of knowledge and evidence; every valid claim to knowledge, it is supposed, will satisfy certain *empirical* criteria; and these criteria, it is then concluded, may be used to determine the extent of our knowledge. Empiricism emphasizes that we proceed slowly upon the basis of experience. But paradoxically—in assuming that we have an answer to the second of our two questions—it begins with a general premise. But if Hume is right, a consistent application of these criteria indicates that we know next to nothing about ourselves and about the physical objects around us.

And so some would begin with an answer to the second question and then attempt to answer the first. Thus it is characteristic of "common-sensism," as an alternative tradition in the theory of knowledge, to assume that we do know most, if not all, of those things that ordinary people think that they know. G. E. Moore has written: "There is no reason why we should not, in this respect, make our philosophical opinions agree with what we necessarily believe at other times. There is no reason why I should not confidently assert that I do really *know* some external facts, although I cannot prove the assertion except by simply assuming that I do. I am, in fact, as certain of this as of anything; and as reasonably certain of it."[1] If we take this point of view, then we can say, with Thomas Reid, that if empiricism has the consequence that we do not know any of these "external facts," then empiricism, *ipso facto,* is false.

A third point of view, with respect to our pair of questions, is that of "skepticism" or "agnosticism." The skeptic or agnostic does *not* assume at the outset that he has an answer to the first question or that he has an answer to the second. Thus, he is able to conclude: "We do not know what, if anything, we know, and we have no way of deciding, in any particular case, whether or not we know."

Many philosophers, perhaps unwittingly, have taken all three points of view. Thus, a single philosopher may attempt to set out in three different directions at once. First, he will employ what he takes to be his knowledge of external physical things in order to test the adequacy of various possible criteria of knowing; in this case, he begins with a claim to know and not with a criterion. Second, he will employ what he takes to be an adequate criterion of knowing in order to decide whether he knows anything about "other minds"; in this case, he begins with a criterion and not with a claim to know. And third, he will approach the field of ethics without either type of preconception; he will not begin with a criterion and he will not begin with a claim to know. Therefore, he will not arrive at any criterion or at any claim to know.

The point of view in the present book has been that of "common-sensism." Unlike the empiricist, we have not begun with general criteria of knowing. Rather we have attempted to derive criteria of knowing, accommodating those criteria to our prior assumptions about what it is that we do know. And we have rejected skepticism, for we have assumed that our knowledge goes beyond what is directly evident or *a priori.*

There is, of course, an element of arbitrariness involved in accepting any one of these three possible points of view and rejecting the other two. But our view is no more arbitrary than either of the others. And unlike them, it corresponds with what we do know.[2]

One may feel, however, that there is a more satisfactory approach to these questions.

[1] G. E. Moore, *Philosophical Studies* (London: Routledge & Kegan Paul, Ltd., 1922), p. 163.

[2] I have discussed further aspects of these difficult questions in *The Problem of the Criterion,* The Aquinas Lecture, 1973 (Milwaukee: Marquette University Press, 1973).

### 3. "SOURCES" OF KNOWLEDGE

One approach to the question, "How are we to decide, in any particular case, *whether* we know?" is to refer to the "sources" of our knowledge and to say that an ostensible item of knowledge is genuine if, and only if, it is the product of a properly accredited source. Thus, it is traditional in Western philosophy to say that there are four such sources:

1. external perception
2. memory
3. self-awareness (reflection, or inner consciousness)
4. reason

(Self-awareness pertains to what we have been calling the directly evident; and reason is said to be that by means of which we have our *a priori* knowledge of necessity.)

Descartes wrote, for example, that "in the matter of the cognition of facts two things alone have to be considered, ourselves who know and the objects themselves which are to be known. Within us there are four faculties only which we can use for this purpose, viz., understanding, imagination, sense, and memory. . . ."[3] And Thomas Reid said, even more clearly: "Thus the faculties of consciousness, of memory, of external sense, and of reason are all equally the gifts of nature. No good reason can be assigned for receiving the testimony of one of them, which is not of equal force with regard to the others."[4]

The principles of evidence that we have tried to formulate may be looked upon as an acknowledgment of the first three, at least, of these traditional sources. The sentence "I think I perceived that thing to be so and so" expresses the content of self-awareness. But we stated conditions under which thinking that one perceives something to be so and so may be said to confer evidence or reasonableness upon the proposition that something *is* so and so; and in so doing, we acknowledged *perception* as a source of knowing. "I think I remember having perceived that thing to be so and so" also expresses the content of self-awareness. But we stated conditions under which thinking that one remembers having perceived something to be so and so might be said to confer reasonableness or acceptability upon the proposition that something *was* so and so; in so doing, we acknowledged *memory* as a source of knowing. And we have said that the content of *self-awareness* is directly evident.

[3] "Rules for the Direction of the Mind," in *The Philosophical Works of Descartes*, E. S. Haldane and G. R. T. Ross, eds. (London: Cambridge University Press, 1934), p. 35.

[4] *Essays on the Intellectual Powers*, Essay VI, Chapter 4, in *The Works of Thomas Reid*, 4th ed., ed. Sir William Hamilton (London: Longmans, Green & Company, Ltd., 1854), p. 439.

But the appeal to such "sources" leaves us with a kind of puzzlement. If the question "How are we to decide, in any particular case, whether we know?" is seriously intended, then the following reply will hardly suffice: "An ostensible item of knowledge is genuine if, and only if, it is the product of a properly accredited source of knowledge." For such a reply naturally leads to further questions: "How are we to decide whether an ostensible source of knowledge *is* properly accredited?" and "How are we to decide just *what* it is that is yielded by a properly accredited source of knowledge?"

Let us now consider how this general "problem of the criterion" arises in other areas of knowledge.

### 4. "KNOWLEDGE OF RIGHT AND WRONG" AS ONE EXAMPLE

At the risk of some slight oversimplification, let us consider one of the controversial questions of moral philosophy. Do we know any distinctively *moral,* or *ethical,* facts? Or what is the status of the claim to such knowledge? The controversies that such questions involve present us with a pattern that recurs with respect to every disputed area of knowledge.

"Mercy as such is good" and "Ingratitude as such is bad" are examples of distinctively moral, or ethical, sentences. (Alternative expressions for the propositions here intended would be "Mercy is intrinsically good, or good in itself" and "Ingratitude is intrinsically bad, or bad in itself.") It has been held that these sentences express something that we can know to be true; it has also been held that they do not. The controversy that concerns us here arises only after the following point has been agreed upon—namely, that the four traditional sources of knowing (external perception, memory, self-awareness, and reason) do not seem to yield what we have been calling ethical and moral knowledge. Or, to put the matter somewhat more exactly, the controversy presupposes this fact: that if we start with the kind of knowledge that is traditionally attributed to these four sources, we cannot construct either a good deductive argument or a good inductive argument to support such statements as "Mercy as such is good" and "Ingratitude as such is bad." Proceeding from this fact, let us contrast the positions of the moral "intuitionist" (or "dogmatist") and the moral "skeptic" (or "agnostic").

The "intuitionist" will reason in essentially the following way:

(P) We have knowledge of certain ethical facts.

(Q) Experience and reason do not yield such knowledge.

(R) Therefore, there is an additional source of knowledge.

The "skeptic," finding no such additional source of knowledge, reasons with equal cogency in the following way:

(Not-R) There is no source of knowledge other than experience and reason.

(Q) Experience and reason do not yield any knowledge of ethical facts.

(Not-P) Therefore we do not have knowledge of any ethical facts.

The intuitionist and the skeptic agree with respect to the second premise, which states that reason and experience do not yield any knowledge of ethical facts. The intuitionist, however, takes as his first premise the contradictory of the skeptic's conclusion; and the skeptic takes as *his* first premise the contradictory of the intuitionist's conclusion. We could say, therefore, that the skeptic begins with a philosophical generalization ("There is no source of knowledge other than experience and reason") and concludes by denying, with respect to a certain type of fact, or alleged fact, that we have knowledge of that type of fact. The intuitionist, on the other hand, begins by saying that we do have knowledge of the type of fact in question and he concludes by denying the skeptic's philosophical generalization. How is one to choose between the two approaches?

The logic of the two arguments reminds us that there is still another possibility. For if (P) and (Q) imply (R), then not only do (not-R) and (Q) imply (not-P), but also (not-R) and (P) imply (not-Q). Hence, one could also argue in this way:

(Not-R) There is no source of knowledge other than experience and reason.

(P) We have knowledge of certain ethical facts.

(Not-Q) Therefore experience and reason yield knowledge of ethical facts.

The first premise of this new argument is rejected by the intuitionist and accepted by the skeptic; the second premise is rejected by the skeptic and accepted by the intuitionist; and the conclusion is rejected by both the intuitionist and the skeptic.

With this third type of argument, one might be said to reject the *faculty* that is claimed by the intuitionist and yet to accept the intuitionist's claim to *knowledge;* in so doing, one is led to reject the *assessment* of experience and reason common to the intuitionist and the skeptic. One says in effect: "It is true that, starting with those propositions that are traditionally attributed to self-awareness, external perception, memory, and reason, we cannot construct any good *inductive* or *deductive* arguments for such propositions as 'Mercy as such is good' and 'Ingratitude is bad.' But from this fact it does not follow that these traditional sources do not yield any knowledge of ethical and moral truths." This is the only possible procedure for one who believes that we do have knowledge of ethical facts and that we do not have a special faculty of moral intuition.

But any such procedure leaves us with a Kantian question: In view of the nature of experience and reason, *how* is such ethical knowledge possible? If we cannot derive the propositions of ethics by applying deduction or induction to the kinds of empirical propositions that we have considered up to now, what is the sense in which experience and reason may yet be said to "yield" our ethical knowledge? There are, I believe, only two possible answers.

One of these may be called "reductive." If we approach the problem "reductively," we attempt to show that the sentences purporting to express our ethical knowledge ("Mercy as such is good" and "Ingratitude as such is bad") can be *translated* or *paraphrased* into empirical sentences that more obviously express the deliverances of experience. Perhaps we will say that "Mercy as such is good" really means the same as "I approve of mercy," or "Most of the people in our culture circle approve of mercy," or "Merciful actions tend to make people happy." Then, by adding the result of such a reductive analysis to the premises of experience and reason, one may hope to produce good inductive or deductive arguments for the propositions expressed by "Mercy as such is good" and "Ingratitude is bad."

But these attempted reductions are entirely implausible; the sentences expressing our ostensible ethical knowledge *seem* at least to express considerably more than is expressed by any of their ostensible empirical translations. (It should be noted, however, that given the type of reductive analysis that we have cited, ethical sentences *do* express something that is true or false and is thus an appropriate object of propositional knowledge. "I approve of mercy" expresses something that is directly evident, and "Most of the people in our culture circle approve of mercy" expresses the kind of knowledge that we may have of "other minds." But given certain *other* types of reductive analysis, ethical sentences do not express what is true or false and therefore do not express anything capable of knowledge. Thus it is held that such sentences, though in the indicative mood, are actually expressions of imperatives or commands. According to this type of view, "Mercy as such is good" might be put in some one of the following ways: "Be merciful!" "Approve of mercy!" "Mercy is to be commended." We will call such theories instances of ethical skepticism, since they do imply that the ethical sentences in question do not express anything that is capable of being known.)

If none of the views expressed so far is acceptable, there is still one more type of answer. We will call it "critical cognitivism." If we are "critical cognitivists," we will *not* say that there are empirical sentences that might serve as translations of the sentences expressing our ethical knowledge; but we will say that there are empirical truths which *enable us to know* certain truths of ethics. Or to use our earlier expression, we will say that the truths of ethics are "known through" certain facts of experience. The latter will then be said to be *signs,* or *criteria,* of the ethical truths. The evil of ingratitude, for example, does not lie in the fact that I do happen to detest it; but the fact that I happen to detest it, or at least the fact that I happen to detest it under certain conditions that can be identified, serves to make known to me the fact that ingratitude *is* something that is evil. My own feeling is a *sign* of the evil nature of ingratitude, and so it could be said to *confer evidence upon* the statement that ingratitude is evil. This point of view is typical of "value-theory" in the Austrian tradition, where *das Wertgefühle,* our feeling for what is intrinsically valuable—for what is good, bad, or neutral in itself—is said to be something we know by means of our "inner consciousness," as well as that which makes known to us what is valuable and what is not.

"Critical cognitivism" will hardly be acceptable to the intuitionist or the skeptic, but there are two points to be made in its favor.

The first point to be made in favor of "critical cognitivism" is that it is a consequence of premises, each of which, when taken separately, seems to be acceptable, if not reasonable. For the critical cognitivist may well say: "We do know that mercy is good and that ingratitude is bad. The sentences in which such truths are expressed are not inductive or deductive consequences of sentences expressing our perceptions, our memories of our perceptions, or our own psychological states; nor can they be translated or paraphrased into such sentences. Yet we have no moral intuitions; experience and reason are our only sources of knowledge. Hence, there must be some empirical truths which serve to make known the facts of ethics. And these truths can only be those that pertain to our feelings for what is good and what is evil."

There is a second point that the "critical cognitivist" may make. He may remind us that the analogue of his critical cognitivism is the most reasonable approach to another, less controversial, area of knowledge. He will be referring to our knowledge of external, physical things—for example, to our knowledge, on a particular occasion, that a cat is on the roof.

### 5. "KNOWLEDGE OF EXTERNAL THINGS" AS ANOTHER EXAMPLE

We have seen that from directly evident premises—premises expressing our awareness of sensations and of our own states of mind—neither induction nor deduction will yield the conclusion "A cat is on the roof." There are at least four different ways in which we might react to this fact.

1. The "intuitionist" will conclude that we have still another source of knowledge, namely, that we know external things not through our "self-presenting states," but by means of some other type of experience. But no such experience is to be found.

2. The "skeptic" will infer that we cannot know, on any occasion, that a cat is on the roof. But we know that he is mistaken.

3. The "reductionist" will infer that "A cat is on the roof" can be translated or paraphrased into sentences expressing one's self-awareness—more particularly, into sentences about the ways in which one is appeared to. To see the implausibility of the reductivist point of view, we have only to ask ourselves *what* appearance sentences—what sentences of the form "I am appeared to in such and such a way"—could possibly express what it is that we know when we know that a cat is on the roof. (The principal difficulty standing in the way of "phenomenalism"—the technical term for this type of reductionism—may be traced to perceptual relativity—to the fact that the ways in which a thing will appear depend not only upon the properties of the thing, but also upon the conditions under which it is perceived and upon the state of the perceiver. Since it is the joint operation of the things we perceive with the conditions under which we perceive them that determines the ways in which the things will appear, we cannot correlate any group of appearances with any particular physical fact, say, a cat being on the roof, unless we refer to some *other* physical fact—the state of the medium and of the perceiver. Trying to define the particular physical fact by reference to appearances alone is not unlike trying to define "uncle" in terms of "descendent" alone and without the use of "male" or "female.")[5]

4. The "critical cognitivist" will take the course we tried to sketch in Chapter 4. He will say that there are principles of induction and deduction, which will tell us, for example, under what conditions the state we have called "thinking that one perceives" tends to confer reasonableness, or tends to confer acceptability, upon the propositions about the past.

**6. "OTHER MINDS"** Another version of the problem of the criterion concerns our knowledge of "other minds." Each of us knows various things about the thoughts, feelings, and purposes of

[5] For further details see C. I. Lewis, "Professor Chisholm and Empiricism," *Journal of Philosophy,* XLV (1948), 517–524; Roderick Firth, "Radical Empiricism and Perceptual Relativity," *Philosophical Review,* LIX (1950), 164–183, 319–331; and Roderick M. Chisholm, *Perceiving: A Philosophical Study* (Ithaca: Cornell University Press, 1957), pp. 189–197. The three articles cited are reprinted in *Perceiving, Sensing, and Knowing,* ed. Robert J. Swartz (Garden City, N.Y.: Doubleday and Company, Inc., 1965). For a defense of one version of phenomenalism, see James Cornman, "Theoretical Phenomenalism," *Nous,* VII (1973), 120–138.

other people; we may be able to say, for example, "I know that Jones is thinking about a horse" or "I know that he is feeling somewhat depressed." Perhaps we will justify our claims to such knowledge by reference, in part, to our perception of certain physical facts which we take to manifest or express the thoughts and feelings in question ("I can see it in his eyes and in the way in which he clenches his teeth, and I can hear it in the sound of his voice"); or we may even justify them by reference to our own feelings of *Verstehen,* or "intuitive understanding" (". . . we know a creature's angry by the way we have felt when we have acted rather as he is acting").[6] The philosopher may then ask: What justification is there for believing that if a man looks and acts in such and such a way or if he leaves me with such and such a feeling then he is either thinking about a horse or he is feeling somewhat depressed?

It is common to suppose that such knowledge is yielded by the traditional "sources" listed above. We know about the thoughts and feelings of other people, it is supposed, in virtue of the knowledge that is yielded by (1) our perception of external things, and in particular, our perception of our own bodies and of the bodies of other people, (2) our immediate awareness of our own thoughts and feelings, (3) our memories of things we come to know by means of such perceptions and states of awareness, and (4) the application of "reason" to the things that we know in these various ways. But how, precisely, can this material be made to yield any knowledge of the thoughts and feelings of other people?

One may be tempted to answer this question by appealing to an enumerative induction. "More often than not, when a man makes a gesture of such and such a sort, he is feeling depressed; this man is now making a gesture of that sort; therefore, in all probability, he is depressed." Or, "More often than not, when Jones rides by those fields he is reminded of the horse that he once owned; he is riding by them now and has a look of fond recollection in his eye; therefore, in all probability, he is thinking about his horse again." But this type of answer obviously does not solve our philosophical problem. For the instances to which we appeal when we make our induction ("He made this gesture yesterday when he was depressed" or "The last time he was here he thought about a horse") presuppose the general type of knowledge-claim we are now trying to justify ("What is your justification for thinking you know that he *was* thinking about a horse that day?").

If we are not to presuppose the type of knowledge-claim that we are trying to justify, then our argument must be an instance of "hypothetical

[6] The second quotation is from John Wisdom, *Other Minds* (Oxford: Basil Blackwell, 1952), p. 194.

induction." The "hypothesis" that Jones is now depressed, or that he is thinking about a horse, will be put forward as the most likely explanation of certain other things we know—presumably, certain facts about Jones's present behavior and demeanor. But in order to construct an inductive argument in which the hypothesis that Jones is depressed, or that he is thinking about a horse, *is* thus to be confirmed, we must have access to a premise telling us what some of the consequences of Jones's depression, or some of the consequences of his thinking about a horse, are likely to be. And how are we to justify *this* premise if we are not entitled to make use of any information about Jones's depression or thoughts?

The only possible way of finding the premise that our hypothetical induction thus requires is to appeal to still another induction—this time an argument from analogy. (Those who argue that there is life on Venus appeal to the "positive analogy" between Venus and the earth—the properties the two planets have in common. Those who argue that there is no life on Venus appeal to the "negative analogy"—the respects in which the two planets differ.) Thus, we might argue: "Jones and I have such and such physical characteristics in common; usually, as a result of being depressed, I will speak in such and such a tone of voice; therefore, in all probability, if Jones is depressed he will also speak in that tone of voice; and he *is* speaking in that tone of voice." Or we might argue: "Jones and I have such and such physical characteristics in common; most of the time, when I think about a horse, I will say 'Yes' if stimulated by the words 'Are you thinking about a horse?'; therefore, in all probability, Jones's thinking about a horse would predispose *him* to say 'Yes' if he were stimulated by the words 'Are you thinking about a horse?' Jones has been stimulated by those words and he *does* say 'Yes.' " We are supposing that the first premise in each of these arguments appeals to a certain positive analogy obtaining between Jones and me. But we must not forget that whoever Jones may be, there is also an impressive negative analogy—difference in background, environment, heredity, physique, and general physiology—and that one could go on *ad indefinitum* enumerating such differences. If we are not entitled to begin with premises referring to Jones's states of mind, it will be very difficult indeed to assess the relative importance of the various points of analogy and disanalogy. Any such analogical argument, therefore, is certain to be weak. Yet we are supposing it is only by means of such an analogical argument that we can justify one of the premises of the hypothetical induction we now proceed to make—either the premise stating "If Jones is depressed, he will speak in such and such a tone of voice" or "If Jones is thinking about a horse he will say 'Yes' if stimulated by 'Are you thinking about a horse?' " Our hypothetical induction, in turn, will yield "Jones is depressed now" or "Jones is thinking about a horse" as being the most likely diagnosis of Jones's present behavior and demeanor.

However, if this procedure is the best that we have, then there is very little, if anything, that we can be said to *know* about the states of minds of other people.

And this fact leads us, once again, to the characteristic argument of the "intuitionist." Perception, memory, and "self-awareness," he will tell us, do not suffice to justify what it is that we claim to know about the states of mind of other people, for no deductive or inductive argument based upon the data of perception, memory, and "self-awareness" will warrant any claim to such knowledge; hence, there must be another source—possibly the *Verstehen,* or "intuitive understanding," of German philosophy and psychology.[7] The intuitionist's point would not be merely that in *Verstehen,* or intuitive understanding, we have a fruitful source of hypotheses about the mental states of other people (presumably there is no one who doubts the practical utility of this faculty); the intuitionist's point would pertain to justification. Thus he might hold, for example, that the fact that a statement expresses one's *Verstehen* will confer reasonableness upon that statement.

The "intuitionist," then, will reason as he did in moral philosophy:

(P) We have knowledge of the states of mind of other people (for example, I know that Jones is thinking about a horse).

(Q) Such knowledge is not yielded by perception, memory, or "self-awareness."

(R) Therefore, there is still another source of knowledge.

The three statements constituting this argument also yield the "skeptical" argument of the philosophical behaviorist:

(Not-R) There is no source of knowledge other than perception, memory, and "self-awareness."

(Q) Knowledge of the states of mind of other people is not yielded by perception, memory, or "self-awareness."

(Not-P) Therefore, we do not have knowledge of the states of mind of other people.[8]

[7] The emphasis upon *Verstehen* as a source of knowledge may be traced to Wilhelm Dilthey's *Einleitung in die Geisteswissenschaften* (Leipzig: Tuebner, 1883), and to the writings of Max Scheler; see Alfred Schuetz, "Scheler's Theory of Intersubjectivity," *Philosophy and Phenomenological Research,* II (1942), 323–341.

[8] Cf. J. B. Watson, *The Ways of Behaviorism* (New York: W. W. Norton & Company, Inc., 1928), pp. 3, 7: "The behaviorist has nothing to say of 'consciousness.' How can

As in the dispute about moral philosophy, the intuitionist and the skeptic agree with respect to the second premise; the intuitionist takes as his first premise the contradictory of the skeptic's conclusion; and the skeptic takes as *his* first premise the contradictory of the intuitionist's conclusion. There is one more possibility:

(Not-R) There is no source of knowledge other than perception, memory, and "self-awareness."

(P) We have knowledge of the states of mind of other people (for example, I know that Jones is thinking about a horse).

(Not-Q) Therefore perception, memory, and "self-awareness" yield this knowledge.

Once again, we are presented with the question "*How* do perception, memory, and inner consciousness yield this knowledge?" and as before we may choose between two answers.

The "reductivist" will tell us that sentences ostensibly concerning the thoughts and feelings of other people ("Jones is thinking about a horse") can be translated or paraphrased into sentences about the bodies of these people. But "reductivism" is no more plausible here than it was in the other cases. To see that this is so, we have only to ask ourselves: *What* sentences about Jones's body could possibly express what it is that we know when we know that Jones is thinking about a horse?

And the "critical cognitivist" will tell us that there are things we can know about a man's body and his behavior that will confer evidence, or reasonableness, upon propositions about these thoughts and feelings; he may add, in deference to *Verstehen,* that certain mental states of our own, which come into being when we are in the presence of others, confer reasonableness, or acceptability, upon propositions about the thoughts and feelings of others.

According to Thomas Reid's version of critical cognitivism, "certain features of the countenance, sounds of the voice, and gestures of the body, indicate certain thoughts and dispositions of mind." Reid's view is, in part, a view about the genesis of our knowledge (he refers, for example, to the way in which children acquire their beliefs). But it is also a theory of evidence—an account of what it is that confers evidence

he? Behaviorism is a natural science. He has neither seen, smelled, nor tasted consciousness nor found it taking part in any human reactions. How can he talk about it until he finds it in his path? . . . Behaviorism's challenge to introspective psychology was: 'You say there is such a thing as consciousness, that consciousness goes on in you—then prove it. You say that you have sensations, perceptions, and images—then demonstrate them as other sciences demonstrate their facts.' " The consistent behaviorist, of course, would also attempt to avoid the facts of "self-awareness."

upon statements about other minds—and as such, it is worth quoting in detail:

> When we see the sign, and see the thing signified always conjoined with it, experience may be the instructor, and teach us how that sign is to be interpreted. But how shall experience instruct us when we see the sign only, when the thing signified is invisible? Now, this is the case here: the thoughts and passions of the mind, as well as the mind itself, are invisible, and therefore their connection with any sensible sign cannot be first discovered by experience; there must be some earlier source of this knowledge. Nature seems to have given to men a faculty or sense, by which this connection is perceived. And the operation of this sense is very analogous to that of the external senses.
>
> When I grasp an ivory ball in my hand, I feel a certain sensation of touch. In the sensation there is nothing external, nothing corporeal. The sensation is neither round nor hard; it is an act of feeling of mind, from which I cannot by reasoning, infer the existence of any body. But, by the constitution of my nature, the sensation carries along with it the conception and belief of a round hard body really existing in my hand. In like manner, when I see the features of an expressive face, I see only figure and colour variously modified. But by the constitution of my nature, the visible object brings along with it the conception and belief of a certain passion or sentiment in the mind of the person.
>
> In the former case, a sensation of touch is the sign, and the hardness and roundness of the body I grasp is signified by that sensation. In the latter case, the features of the person is the sign, and the passion or sentiment is signified by it.[9]

**7. A FINAL EXAMPLE** Knowledge, or ostensible knowledge, of God and of what some take to be theological truths, provides us with a final illustration of the problem of the criterion. Perhaps we are now in a position to understand the type of impasse to which the various possible points of view give rise; therefore, perhaps we can express these points of view much more simply than any of their proponents can.

The "dogmatist" or "intuitionist" will argue that (P) we *do* have knowledge of the existence of God and of other theological facts; but (Q) this knowledge is not yielded, or significantly confirmed by, anything that is yielded by reason or experience; hence, (R) there is a source of knowledge in addition to reason and experience. Thus, Hugh of St. Victor held, in the twelfth century, that in addition to the *oculis carnis,* by means of which we know the physical world, and the *oculis rationis,*

[9] *Essays on the Intellectual Powers of Man,* Essay VI, Chapter 5, in *The Works of Thomas Reid,* pp. 449–450. Of the types of "sign" distinguished in the first two sentences of this passage, the Stoics called the first "commemorative" and the second "indicative"; Sextus Empiricus, as a skeptic, held that there are no "indicative signs." See Sextus Empiricus, *Against the Logicians,* Book II, Chapter 3, in Vol. II of *Sextus Empiricus,* The Loeb Classical Library (Cambridge: Harvard University Press, 1933), pp. 313–397.

by means of which we know our own states of mind, there is also an *oculis contemplationis,* by means of which we know the truth of religion.[10]

Finding no such contemplative eye, the "agnostic"—the theological skeptic—argues that (not-R) reason and experience are the only sources of knowledge; (Q) reason and experience do not supply any information, or significantly confirm any hypothesis, about the existence of God or about any other theological facts; hence, (not-P) we have no knowledge about God.

And the third possibility is to argue that (not-R) there is no source of knowledge other than experience and reason; (P) we have knowledge of the existence of God and of certain other theological facts; hence, (not-Q) experience and reason do supply us with information about the existence of God and other theological facts.

Before taking refuge in "reductionism" or "critical cognitivism," the theist may explore the possibilities of using induction and deduction in order to derive the truths in question from the deliverances of the *oculis carnis* and the *oculis rationis.* We will not consider these possibilities here, for they take us beyond the questions of the theory of knowledge. But, so far as the theory of knowledge is concerned, it is instructive to consider the relative merits of (1) proving the existence of God from the facts of nature, (2) proving the existence of external things from the ways in which we are appeared to, and (3) proving the existence of other people's states of mind from facts about their behavior. But many theists who are not skeptics have doubts about the traditional proofs, and for them, the alternatives are "reductionism" and "critical cognitivism."[11]

"Reductionism" seems to be exemplified in contemporary Protestant theology. The cognitive content of such sentences as "God exists" is thought to be expressible in sentences about the thoughts, feelings, and behavior of religious people. To see the implausibility of reductionism, we have only to ask ourselves, as before: *What* sentences about the thoughts, feelings, and behavior of religious people can possibly express what it is that the religious man thinks he knows when he thinks he knows that God exists?

Finally, "critical cognitivism" would be the view that what we know about God is "known through" certain other things in precisely the way in which the content of other types of knowledge are "known through"

10 See Maurice De Wulf, *History of Mediaeval Philosophy,* I (London: Longmans, Green & Company, Ltd., 1935), p. 214.

11 Compare: Chapters 2 and 5 in John Hick, *Philosophy of Religion,* 2nd ed. (Englewood Cliffs, N.J.: Prentice-Hall, Inc., 1973); and Alvin Plantinga, *God and Other Minds* (Ithaca: Cornell University Press, 1967).

the directly evident, or known through what is itself known through the directly evident. Just what the facts are that may be said to confer reasonableness, or acceptability, upon the ostensible truths of religion would seem to be problematic. But given such facts, whether they pertain to sacred writings, the sayings of religious teachers, or one's experience of "the Holy," the critical cognitivist may distinguish, as theologians do, between *exegesis* and *hermeneutics,* the former being an account of just what these facts are, and the latter, an account of the types of proposition upon which they may be said to confer evidence, reasonableness, or acceptability. Our account of the directly evident in Chapter 2 might similarly be said to be a matter of exegesis, and our account of the indirectly evident in Chapter 3 a matter of hermeneutics.

It may not be surprising, then, that the general problem of the criterion has created impasses in almost every branch of knowledge. I am afraid that I can throw no further light upon the problem itself; but if we can appreciate its difficulties, perhaps we will better understand some of the controversies that are involved in the topics of the preceding chapters.[12]

[12] I have discussed the general problem from a somewhat different point of view in *The Problem of the Criterion,* The Aquinas Lecture, 1973 (Milwaukee: Marquette University Press, 1973).

# APPENDIX: DEFINITIONS AND PRINCIPLES

## 1. LIST OF DEFINITIONS

The definitions formulated in Chapter 1 make use of (i) the concepts of logic, (ii) the concept of belief or acceptance, and (iii) that of epistemic preferability, expressible in the locution "*p* is more reasonable than *q* for *S* at *t*." For simplicity, the temporal reference is omitted from most definitions.

D1.1 *h* is *beyond reasonable doubt* for *S* =Df Accepting *h* is more reasonable for *S* than is withholding *h*.

The expression "withholding *h*" may be taken to abbreviate "not believing *h* and not believing not-*h*."

D1.2 *h* has *some presumption in its favor* for *S* =Df Accepting *h* is more reasonable for *S* than accepting not-*h*.

D1.3 *h* is *acceptable* for *S* =Df Withholding *h* is not more reasonable for *S* than accepting *h*.

D1.4 *h* is *certain* for *S* =Df *h* is beyond reasonable doubt for *S*, and there is no *i* such that accepting *i* is more reasonable for *S* than accepting *h*.

D1.5 *h* is *evident* for *S* =Df (i) *h* is beyond reasonable doubt for *S* and (ii) for every *i*, if accepting *i* is more reasonable for *S* than accepting *h*, then *i* is certain for *S*.

The following definition may be added to those that were listed in Chapter 1:

D1.6 *h* is *counterbalanced* for *S* =Df Accepting *h* is not more reasonable for *S* than accepting not-*h*, and accepting not-*h* is not more reasonable for *S* than accepting *h*.

An additional undefined concept is introduced in the definitions that immediately follow. This is the concept of *de re necessity,* expressible in the locution "*x* is necessarily such that it is *F*."

D2.1 *h* is *self-presenting* for *S* at *t* =Df *h* occurs at *t;* and necessarily, if *h* occurs at *t*, then *h* is evident for *S* at *t*.

An alternative formulation of D2.1 is

> *h* is self-presenting for *S* at *t* =Df *h* is true at *t;* and necessarily if *h* is true at *t,* then *h* is evident for *S* at *t.*

D2.2 *h* is *directly evident* for *S* =Df *h* is logically contingent; and there is an *e* such that (i) *e* is self-presenting for *S* and (ii) necessarily, whoever accepts *e* accepts *h.*

The expression "*h* is logically contingent" abbreviates "It is false that *h* is necessarily such that it obtains and it is also false that *h* is necessarily such that it does not obtain."

D3.1 *h* is an *axiom* =Df *h* is necessarily such that (i) it is true and (ii) for every *S,* if *S* accepts *h,* then *h* is certain for *S.*

D3.2 *h* is *axiomatic* for *S* =Df (i) *h* is an axiom and (ii) *S* accepts *h.*

D3.3 *h* is known *a priori* by *S* =Df There is an *e* such that (i) *e* is axiomatic for *S,* (ii) the proposition, *e* implies *h,* is axiomatic for *S,* and (iii) *S* accepts *h.*

D3.4 *h* is *a priori* =Df It is possible that there is someone for whom *h* is *a priori.*

D4.1 *e tends to confirm h* =Df Necessarily, for every *S,* if *e* is evident for *S* and if everything that is evident for *S* is entailed by *e,* then *h* has some presumption in its favor for *S.*

The following is an alternative to D4.1:

> *e tends to confirm h* =Df Necessarily, for every *S,* if either (a) *e* is evident for *S* and such that everything that is evident for *S* is entailed by *e* or (b) *e* is indirectly evident for *S* and such that everything that is indirectly evident for *S* is entailed by *e,* then *h* has some presumption in its favor for *S.*

The expression "*e* is indirectly evident for *S*" may here be taken to abbreviate "*h* is evident for *S* but neither directly evident nor *a priori* for *S.*"

D4.2 *i defeats* the confirmation that *e* tends to provide for *h* =Df (i) *e* tends to confirm *h,* and (ii) the conjunction, *e* and *i,* does not tend to confirm *h.*

D4.3 *S* believes, *without ground for doubt,* that *p* =Df (i) *S* believes that *p* and (ii) no conjunction of propositions that are acceptable for *S* tends to confirm the negation of the proposition that *p.*

Definition D4.3, unlike those that precede it, is schematic; the letter "*p*" may be replaced by any English declarative sentence. "*S* believes that *p*" could be replaced by "the state of affairs that *p* is accepted by *S*."

D4.4 *A* is a set of *concurrent* propositions =Df *A* is a set of two or more propositions each of which is such that the conjunction of all the others tends to confirm it and is logically independent of it.

The use of "entails" and "logically independent" in the foregoing call for two additional definitions:

D4.5 *e entails h* =Df *e* is necessarily such that (i) if it obtains then *h* obtains and (ii) whoever accepts it accepts *h*.

D4.6 *e* is *logically independent* of *h* =Df *e* is necessarily such that (i) it does not entail *h*, (ii) it does not entail the negation of *h*, (iii) it is not entailed by *h*, and (iv) it is not entailed by the negation of *h*.

The definitions suggested in Chapter 5 may be put somewhat more formally as follows.

D5.1 *h* is a *state of affairs* =Df It is possible that there is someone who accepts *h*.

D5.2 *h* is a *proposition* =Df *h* is a state of affairs which is necessarily such that either it always obtains or it never obtains.

The undefined expression "obtains" may be replaced by "occurs" or "takes place."

D5.3 *h* is *true* =Df *h* is a state of affairs that obtains.

D5.4 *h* is a *fact* =Df *h* is a state of affairs that obtains.

D5.5 *S* has a *true belief de dicto* =Df *S* accepts a state of affairs that obtains.

"False" may replace "true" in the above, provided "does not obtain" replaces "obtains."

The next definition introduces the concepts of *having a property* and of *attributing a property to something.*

D5.6 *S* has a *true belief de re* =Df There is something *x* and a property *P* such that (i) *x* has *P* and (ii) *S* attributes *P* to *x*.

"False" may replace "true," provided "*x* has *P*" is replaced by "*x* does not have *P*."[1]

The following definition makes use of the concept of a sentence-token and that of a sentence-token *expressing* a state of affairs *in* a language.

[1] A way of reducing belief *de re* to belief *de dicto* is suggested in the author's "Knowledge and Belief: 'De Dicto' and 'De Re,'" *Philosophical Studies,* 33 (1975), 9–28.

D5.7 *T* is a sentence-token that is true in *L* =Df *T* is a sentence-token and there is a state of affairs *h* such that (i) *T* expresses *h* in *L* and (ii) *h* obtains.

"False" may replace "true," provided "*h* does not obtain" replaces "*h* obtains."

D6.1 *e* is a *basis* of *h* for *S* =Df *e* is self-presenting for *S;* and necessarily, if *e* is self-presenting for *S,* then *h* is evident for *S.*

D6.2 *e confers evidence* upon *h* for *S* =Df *e* is evident for *S;* and every *b* such that *b* is a basis of *e* for *S* is a basis of *h* for *S.*

D6.3 *h* is *nondefectively evident* for *S* =Df Either *h* is certain for *S,* or *h* is evident for *S* and is entailed by a conjunction of propositions each having for *S* a basis which is not a basis of any false proposition for *S.*

D6.4 *h* is *known* by *S* =Df *h* is accepted by *S; h* is true; and *h* is nondefectively evident for *S.*

D6.5 *e* is evidence *S* has for *h* =Df Either (i) *e* is identical with *h* and is directly evident or *a priori* for *S* or (ii) *e* does not imply *h* but confers evidence upon *h* for *S.*

The following definition was also suggested in Chapter 6:

D6.6 *h* is in the absolute sense *more probable than not* for *S* =Df There is an *e* such that (i) *e* is known by *S,* (ii) *e* tends to confirm *h,* and (iii) there is no *i* such that *i* is known by *S* and the conjunction of *e* and *i* does not tend to confirm *h.*

## 2. LIST OF PRINCIPLES

In the following statement of the principles of epistemic logic that are referred to in Chapter 1, the expressions "*Bh,*" "*Wh,*" and "*P*" may be taken to abbreviate respectively, "accepting *h,*" "withholding *h,*" and "is more reasonable for *S* at *t* than."

(A1) For every *h* and *i,* if *Bh P Bi,* then *S* understands *h.*

(A2) For every *e, h,* and *i,* if it is false that *Be P Bh,* and if it is false that *Bh P Bi,* then it is false that *Be P Bi.*

(A3) For every *h* and *i,* if *Bh P Bi,* then it is false that *Bi P Bh.*

(A4) For every *h,* if it is false that *Wh P Bh,* then *Bh P B~h.*

The expression "~*h*" may be read as "the negation of *h.*"

(A5) For every *h* and *i, Bh P Bi,* if and only if, *B~i P B~h.*

The letter "*S*" in the following formula may be read as "is the same in epistemic value as"; the locution "*pSq*" abbreviates "*p* is not more reasonable for *S* at *t* than *q*, and *q* is not more reasonable for *S* at *t* than *p*."

(A6) For every *h* and *i*, *Wh S Wi*, if and only if, either *Bh S Bi* or *B~h S Bi*.

(A7) For every *h* and *i*, if *Bi P Bh* and *Bi P B~h*, then *Wh P Wi*.

(A8) *h* is identical with *~~h*.

The final principle, which may be thought of as belonging to the general theory of states of affairs rather than to epistemic logic, enables us to deduce that withholding *h* is the same as withholding the negation of *h*.

The following eight principles of evidence are formulated in Chapter 4.

(A) *S*'s being *F* is such that, if it occurs, then it is self-presenting to *S* that he is *F*.

The predicates that may replace the schematic letter "*F*" in (A) are restricted to those which would yield a description of a self-presenting state.

(B) For any subject *S*, if *S* believes without ground for doubt, that he is perceiving something to be *F*, then it is beyond reasonable doubt for *S* that he perceives something to be *F*.

(C) For any subject *S*, if *S* believes, without ground for doubt, that he is perceiving something to be *F*, then it is evident for *S* that he perceives something to be *F*.

The predicates that may replace "*F*" in (C) are restricted to those connoting sensible characteristics.

(D) For any subject *S*, if *S* believes, without ground for doubt, that he remembers perceiving something to be *F*, then the proposition that he does remember perceiving something to be *F* is one that is acceptable for *S*.

(E) For any subject *S*, if *S* believes, without ground for doubt, that he remembers perceiving something to be *F*, then it is beyond reasonable doubt for *S* that he does remember perceiving something to be *F*.

(F) For any subject *S*, if *S* believes, without ground for doubt, that he remembers being *F*, then it is beyond reasonable doubt for *S* that he does remember that he was *F*.

The predicates that may replace "*F*" in (F) are restricted to those which would yield a description of a self-presenting state.

(G) If the conjunction of all those propositions *e,* such that *e* is acceptable for *S* at *t* tends to confirm *h,* then *h* has some presumption in its favor for *S* at *t.*

(H) Any set of concurring propositions, each of which has some presumption in its favor for *S,* is such that each of its members is beyond reasonable doubt for *S.*

Given definitions D5.1 and D5.2, "proposition" in (G) and (H) could be replaced by "state of affairs."

(I) If *S* believes, without ground for doubt, that he perceives something to be *F,* and if the proposition that there is something that is *F* is a member of a set of concurrent propositions each of which is beyond reasonable doubt for *S,* then it is evident for *S* that he perceives something to be *F.*

The following four principles about knowing that one knows are formulated in Chapter 6.

(K1) If *S* considers the proposition that he knows that *p,* and if it is evident to *S* that *p,* then it is evident to *S* that he knows that *p.*

(K2) If it is evident to *S* that he knows that *p,* and if *S* does not know that *p,* then there is a false proposition which is evident for *S* and which neither implies nor is implied by the proposition that *p.*

(K3) If it is evident to *S* that he knows that *p,* then it is evident to *S* that the result of adding any true proposition to his evidence for *p* either implies *p* or would confer evidence upon *p.*

(K4) If *S* considers the proposition that he knows that *p,* and if he does know that *p,* then he knows that he knows that *p.*

# INDEX


Acceptability, 9–10
Agnosticism, 5–6, 132–34 (*see also* Skepticism)
Agrippa, 9
Albertus Magnus, 95
Alston, William J., 22, 63
Ambrose, Alice, 40–41
Analogy, 128–30
Analytic statements, 54–61
Anderson, Alan R., 104
*A posteriori* knowledge, 36–37, 44, 46–47
Appearing, 26–33
*A priori* knowledge, 34, 113
Aquinas, St. Thomas, 44, 46–61
Aristotle, 18, 28, 37, 38–39, 41–42, 43, 77, 89, 101
Armstrong, D. W., 102
Augustine, St., 7, 27, 70
Austin, J. L., 27
Ayer, A. J., 116
Axioms, 40–46, 85

Bayle, Pierre, 15
Baylis, C. A., 87
Behaviorism, 130–31
Benfield, David, 44
Blanshard, Brand, 99–100
Bochenski, I. M., 47, 95
Bolzano, Bernard, 47, 87, 88, 118
Brentano, Franz, 26, 39, 46, 47, 60, 81, 99–100, 114
Butler, Bishop Joseph, 117–18

Canfield, John, 24
Carnap, Rudolf, 53, 72
Carneades, 67–71, 76–77, 79, 82–83, 118
Certainty, 10–11, 42
Church, Alonzo, 49
Cicero, 71
Coffey, P., 116
"Coherence theory," 63
"Common sensibles," 77
"Commonsensism," 121–34
Concurrence, 69–70, 82–84
Confirmation, 71–73, 82–84
Cornman, James, 127
Counterbalancing, 10, 135
"Critical cognitivism," 125–26

Danto, Arthur, 114
*De dicto* and *de re,* 88–90
Defeat, 72–73, 115–16
Demonstrative knowledge, 114
Descartes, Rene, 18, 26–27, 44, 121
Dewey, John, 98, 115–16
Dilthey, Wilhelm, 130
Donnelan, K. S., 22, 94
Dretske, Fred, 106
Ducasse, C. J., 22

Empiricism, 120–21

Epictetus, 9
Epimenides, 91
Epistemic logic, 13–14, 138–39
Epistemic terms, 5–15, 135–36
Ethics, knowledge of, 123–27
Evidence:
  direct, 2, 16–33, 63–66, 98–99
  indirect, 62–86
  rules of, 62–85
Evident, the, 11–12, 15
Exegesis, 134

Firth, Roderick, 22, 83, 127
Fitch, F. B., 94
"Foundationalism," 63
Frankena, William, 60
Frege, Gottlob, 37, 41, 51, 87

Galis, L., 106
Garver, N., 94
Gettier, Edmund L., 105–10
Ginet, Carl, 116
God, knowledge of, 132–34
Goldman, Alvin, 106
Gratuitousness, 8

Haller, Rudolf, 25
Hanen, Marsha, 71
Harman, Gilbert, 115–17
Heidelberger, Herbert, 75
Hermeneutics, 134
Herzberger, H., 94
Hick, John, 133
Hilpinen, Risto, 115, 116
Hintikka, Jaakko, 115, 116
Holy, the, 132–34
Hugh of St. Victor, 132–33
Husserl, Edmund, 18, 40, 50, 53

Induction, 36–40, 64–67, 103
  intuitive, 38–40
  problem of, 84–85
Instrumentalism, 97–98
Intuitionism, 123–24
"Intuitive understanding," 128–31

James, William, 14, 97–98
Joachim, H. H., 100
Johnsen, Bredo, 106
Johnson, W. E., 38
Jourdain, P. E. B., 51
Justification, 6, 62–64, 85–86

Kant, Immanuel, 45–46, 54–57, 85
Kearns, J., 94
Keim, Robert, 13–14
Keynes, J. M., 71, 118
Körner, Stephan, 14
Kim, Jaegwon, 67
Klein, Peter, 106
Knowing that one knows, 4, 113–18
Kripke, Saul, 117
Kyburg, Henry, 67

Langford, C. H., 59
Lazerowitz, Morris, 40–41
Lehrer, Keith, 63, 83, 96, 102, 106, 117
Leibniz, G. W., 20–21, 22, 30, 33, 34, 40–41, 46, 60, 87–88
Lemmon, E. J., 116
Lewis, C. I., 16–17, 79, 81, 83, 87, 127
"Linguisticism," 53–54
Linsky, L., 61
Lipps, Theodore, 50
Locke, John, 44–45, 60
Lykos, K., 28

Mach, Ernst, 40
Malcolm, Norman, 44
Martin, Robert L., 94
"Meaning postulates," 59–60
Meinong, A., 18, 21, 78, 81, 84, 104
Memory, 79–82
Mercier, D. J., 116
Moody, Ernest, 95
Moore, G. E., 15, 120–21

Necessity, 34–40, 43
Negative apprehension, 23–24
Nelson, Leonard, 18, 26, 49

Other minds, 127–32

Paradoxes, 48, 91–97
Pastin, Mark, 63
Paul, St., 91
Paxon, Thomas, 106
Peirce, C. S., 96, 100
Perception, 66, 68–69, 73–78
Performative utterances, 27
Phenomenalism, 172
Plantinga, Alvin, 133
Plato, 36–37
Pollock, John, 33, 85, 94, 106, 114
Pragmatism, 97–98
Price, H. H., 78, 83
Prichard, H. A., 30, 116
Probability, 71, 117–18, 138
"Proper objects of sense," 28, 77
Properties, 34–36, 40, 88–89
Propositions, 5–6, 22, 35, 82, 87–89, 137
Protestant theology, 133
Proteresthesis, 81
"Psychologism," 50–53
Pyrrho, 10

Quine, W. V., 53, 61
Quinn, Philip L., 14
Quinton, Anthony, 53

Reason (*see* Truth of reason)
Reasonability, 6–9
"Reductivism," 125–34
Reichenbach, Hans, 31
Reid, Thomas, 30, 70, 121, 131–32, 133
Requirement, 14–15
Rescher, Nicholas, 63, 100, 183
Ross, James, 47
Roth, Michael, 106
Russell, Bertrand, 7, 18, 81, 104–5

Salmon, Wesley, 67
Scheler, Max, 130
Schuetz, Alfred, 130
Scotus, Duns, 39
"Self-presenting states," 20–26, 73
Sellars, Wilfrid, 22, 63
Sentences, 89–95
Sextus Empiricus, 9, 10, 19, 28, 67–71, 100, 132
Skepticism, 9, 10, 25–26, 48–50, 83, 121–34
Skyrms, B., 94
Socrates, 18
Socratic questions, 16–21
"Sources of knowledge," 122–23
Sosa, Ernest, 106, 109, 115–16
States of affairs, 5, 22, 35, 82, 87–89, 137
Steel, Thomas, 22
Stevenson, J. T., 14
Stough, Charlotte, 67
Stroll, Avrum, 114, 116
Swain, Marshall, 106
Synthetic *a priori*, 57–60
Synthetic statements, 54–61

Truth, 3–4, 15, 87–97, 137
  of reason, 33–61, 113

Unacceptability, 9
Understanding, 13, 41

van Frassen, B. C., 94
*Verstehen,* 128–31

Watson, J. B., 130–31
Whewell, William, 37
White, Morton, 61
Will, F. L., 63
Wisdom, John, 128
Withholding, 6, 9, 138–39
Wittgenstein, L., 16–17, 25

Xenophon, 18